The Least You Should Know About Vocabulary Building

Second Edition

The Least You Should Know About Vocabulary Building

Word Roots

TERESA FERSTER GLAZIER
Western Illinois University

HOLT, RINEHART AND WINSTON, INC.
New York   Chicago   San Francisco   Philadelphia
Montreal   Toronto   London   Sydney   Tokyo
Mexico City   Rio de Janeiro   Madrid

Library of Congress Cataloging in Publication Data

Glazier, Teresa Ferster.
The least you should know about vocabulary building.

Includes index.
1. Vocabulary.   2. English language—Roots.
3. English language—Word formation.   I. Title.
PE1449.G55   1985   428.1   84-6519

ISBN 0-03-070694-7

Requests for permission to make copies of any
part of the work should be mailed to:
Permissions, Holt, Rinehart and Winston, Inc.,
111 Fifth Avenue, New York, New York 10003
Printed in the United States of America

8   090   9   8   7   6

Holt, Rinehart and Winston
The Dryden Press
Saunders College Publishing

To the Instructor

With its emphasis on word roots, this text will help students begin what should become a lifelong study of words. The following features make it easy to use either in the classroom or for self-help.

1. Since only one approach is used—word roots—students can work through the text easily. They learn a method of study while learning the first root and follow that method throughout the book.
2. The 55 roots included are not invariably the most common but rather the most interesting and the easiest to spot and remember—ones that will help unlock the meaning of new words.
3. No distinction is made between Greek and Latin roots. Students need to remember the meaning of a root rather than its language source.
4. Similarly, no distinction is made among roots, prefixes, and suffixes because all are equally sources of word meaning. All are called word roots—the roots from which our language came.
5. Pronunciation aids are simple, the only diacritical mark being the one for long vowels.
6. Definitions are illustrated in sentences.
7. Under each root the words are listed in approximate order of difficulty unless there is reason for putting words of similar construction together. Some difficult words are included for those who happen to be ready for them, but students should be encouraged to concentrate on words they have encountered before and are curious about.
8. Answers at the back of the book for the exercises allow students to teach themselves.
9. In the second part of the book (beginning on p. 141), 164 additional roots are presented briefly for further study and reference.
10. A Root Index and a Word Index simplify using the text.

T.F.G.

Acknowledgments

The idea for this book I owe to my father from whom I learned the meaning of such words as *propensity, corpulent,* and *commodious* before I could read. I can still hear the creak of the old metal dictionary stand as my father would open the *Funk and Wagnalls New Standard Dictionary* to look up a word and then try the word out again and again on Mother and me. From him I learned to keep word lists and to probe for root meanings. This is really his book.

For careful commentary on the early drafts I am grateful to Jay Balderson, Gretchen Glazier Boyer, Teresa Edwards, Kenneth Glazier, Jr., and Liz Roth. I also appreciate the suggestions from users of the first edition and from reviewers of this edition. And for a most helpful final review I am indebted to Robert W. L. Smith of Mission College, Santa Clara, California.

Contents

The
Least
You
Should
Know
About
Vocabulary
Building

Increasing Your Vocabulary Through Learning Word Roots

How did words get to be words? Why, for example, is a hippopotamus called a hippopotamus and not a glipserticka? There's a good reason. Since the animal looks a bit like a fat horse and spends much of its time in rivers, the Greeks combined their word for horse, HIPPOS, and their word for river, POTAMOS, and called the animal a hippopotamos, a river horse. And with only a one-letter change, the word has come down to us as hippopotamus.

Words did not just happen. They grew. And if you learn how they grew—what original roots they came from—you'll find it easier to remember them. You'll *understand* the words you look up in the dictionary instead of just memorizing the definitions. And weeks later, even though you may have forgotten the meaning of a word, your knowledge of its roots[1] will help you recall its meaning.

Not all words, of course, let their roots show through, and you simply have to look up such words and memorize their meanings. But you can tackle them later.

The best first step in vocabulary building, then, is to become familiar with some word roots because learning the root of one word often gives a clue to dozens or hundreds more. For example, if you learn that SYN (SYM, SYL) means *together* or *with*, you have a clue to more than 450 words, for that many words beginning with SYN (SYM, SYL) are listed in *Webster's Third New International Dictionary*. Similarly, when you learn that *philanthropist* is made up of PHIL *to love* and ANTHROP *human*, you have learned not only that a philanthropist is a lover of humanity, but you also have a clue to some 70 other words beginning with PHIL and to more than 60 others beginning with ANTHROP, not to mention those that have PHIL or ANTHROP in the middle or at the end of the word.

As you become aware of how words are made up, familiar words will take on new meaning, and unfamiliar words may often be understood even without a dictionary. For instance, if you know that the root BIBL means *book* as in *bibliography* and *Bible*, then you can guess that a *bibliophile* will have something to do with books. And if you remember that PHIL means *to love*, as in *philanthropist* (lover of humanity) and *philosophy*

---

[1] In this book the term roots includes prefixes and suffixes because all word parts are equally sources of word meaning. All are the roots from which our language came.

1

(love of wisdom), then you will immediately guess that a bibliophile must be a lover of books.

Glancing at the root chain below will help you spot some common roots. The chain begins with *biped* [BI two + PED foot], a two-footed animal. The next word contains one of the preceding roots, PED. A *pedometer* [PED foot + METER measure] is, as its roots indicate, a "foot measure" or an instrument that measures the distance walked by recording the number of steps taken. The next word must contain METER, and out of the hundreds of METER words, *geometry* [GEO earth + METER measure] has been chosen. As its roots show, geometry was originally a system of "earth measuring," that is, of measuring the earth through the use of angles. The next word must contain GEO, and so on.

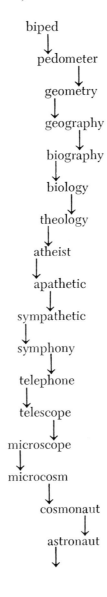

astronomy

↓

autonomy

↓

automobile

↓

immobile

↓

infidel

↓

confident

↓

committee

↓

transmit

↓

transport

↓

report

↓

recur

↓

excursion

↓

exclude

↓

seclude

↓

secure

↓

manicure

↓

manuscript

↓

subscribe

↓

subversive

↓

controversy

↓

contradict

↓

benediction

↓

benefactor

↓

facilitate

This root chain ends with *facilitate*. Perhaps reading the chain may facilitate your noticing word roots in the future.

After you've learned some of the roots in this book, try to make a root chain of your own. You'll be surprised how one root leads to another.

Learning word roots is not only the quickest way to increase your vocabulary but also the most entertaining. For example, did you know . . .

that **salary** [SAL salt] originally was the money paid to Roman soldiers to buy salt . . .

that a **companion** [COM with + PAN bread] was originally a person one shared one's bread with . . .

that **malaria** [MAL bad + AER air] was so named because people thought it was caused by the bad air of the swamps . . .

that a **terrier** [TERR earth] got its name because it digs in the earth after small animals in burrows . . .

that **escape** [ES out + CAP cape] originally meant to get out of one's cape, leaving it in the hands of the pursuer . . .

that an **insect** [IN in + SECT to cut] was so named because its body is "cut" into three segments . . .

that a **bonfire** in the Middle Ages was the bone fire built to dispose of corpses during the plague . . .

that **panic** originally described the frantic efforts of the Greek nymphs to escape when the mischievous god Pan suddenly appeared among them . . .

that **curfew** in the Middle Ages in France was the ringing of a bell called the *couvre-feu* or cover fire, which told the peasants to cover or extinguish their fires for the night . . .

that **alphabet** comes from the first two letters of the Greek alphabet, ALPHA and BETA, "a" and "b" . . .

that a **pedagogue** [PED child + AGOG leader] was originally a slave who led a Greek child to school . . .

that **precocious** [PRE before + COQUERE to cook] originally meant cooked before time . . .

that **trivia** [TRI three + VIA way] in Roman times meant the crossroads where three ways met and where women on their way to market stopped to chat about unimportant things (TRI VIA talk) . . .

Other interesting word stories will be uncovered as you trace words back to their origins.

Where to Find Word Roots in Your Dictionary

Most dictionaries give the derivation of words. You'll find the derivation either just after or just before the definition.

The American Heritage Dictionary, Second College Edition[1]

> **eu·pho·ny** (yōō'fə-nē) *n., pl.* **-nies**. Agreeable sound, esp. in the phonetic quality of words. [Fr. *euphonie* < LLat. *euphonia* < Gk. < *euphōnos*, sweet-voiced : *eu*-, good + *phōnē*, sound.]

The derivation is in square brackets at the end of the definition. The last part of the derivation gives the original roots and their meanings: *eu*-, good + *phone*, sound.

Webster's New World Dictionary, Second College Edition[2]

> **eu·pho·ny** (-nē) *n., pl.* **-nies** [Fr. *euphonie* < LL. *euphonia* < Gr. *euphōnia* < *euphōnos*, sweet-voiced, musical < *eu*-, well + *phōnē*, voice: see PHONE¹] the quality of having a pleasing sound; pleasant combination of agreeable sounds in spoken words; also, such a combination of words

The derivation is in square brackets before the definition. The last part of the derivation gives the original roots and their meanings: *eu*-, well + *phone*, voice.

Webster's Ninth New Collegiate Dictionary[3]

> **eu·pho·ny** \'yü-fə-nē\ *n, pl* **-nies** [F *euphonie*, fr. LL *euphonia*, fr. Gk *euphōnia*, fr. *euphōnos* sweet-voiced, musical, fr. *eu*- + *phōnē* voice — more at BAN] (ca. 1623) **1 :** pleasing or sweet sound; *esp* **:** the acoustic effect produced by words so formed or combined as to please the ear **2 :** a harmonious succession of words having a pleasing sound —

The derivation is in square brackets before the definition. The last part of the derivation gives the original roots and the meaning of one of them: *phone*, voice. To find the meaning of the other root, look for *eu*- as a regular dictionary entry. There its meaning is given: well or good.

Thus the roots indicate that *euphony* must mean good sound. And when you look at the definitions, you'll discover that that is exactly what it means: agreeable sound; the quality of having a pleasing sound; pleasing or sweet sound. Having learned the roots of *euphony*, you'll remember the word longer than if you had merely looked up the definition.

Changes in Root Spelling

A root may change its spelling slightly according to the word it is in. For example, EX *out* is found in **excursion,** but it changes to ES in **escape** and to simply E in **educate.** Such changes have occurred to make pronunciation easier. Escape and educate are easier to pronounce than excape and exducate would be. Here are some of the ways root spellings change.

Sometimes the last letter of a root changes to be like the first letter of the root that follows:

COM nect	becomes	CON nect
COM loquial	becomes	COL loquial
COM relate	becomes	COR relate
DIS fident	becomes	DIF fident
SYN metrical	becomes	SYM metrical

Sometimes the last letter of a root changes (or is dropped) to make the pronunciation easier, but it doesn't become the same as the first letter of the root that follows:

EX cape	becomes	ES cape
COM temporary	becomes	CON temporary
SYN pathy	becomes	SYM pathy
DIS vert	becomes	DI vert
EX ducate	becomes	E ducate

A root may also appear in slightly different forms in different words. CLUD, *to close, to shut,* may appear as

CLUD	in	seclude
CLUS	in	recluse
CLAUS	in	claustrophobia
CLOS	in	closet

but you'll soon learn to spot a root even when its spelling varies.

How to Use This Book

The roots in this text are presented alphabetically because it makes little difference which one you study first.

Under many roots (for example, see ANN, ENN) two lists of words are given. The first list has common words not requiring pronunciation helps or sentence examples. The second list includes more difficult words. Don't try to learn them all. Skip the unfamiliar ones. They're included merely for anyone who happens to be ready for them. Concentrate on words you've heard or seen before and wondered about, words you almost know but aren't quite sure of. They're the ones you can learn most easily. And mastering even a few words under each root will give quite a boost to your vocabulary.

Here are six steps to take as you begin your study.

1. First, take the preliminary test on page 9. Later you'll have a chance to take a similar test to see how the study of word roots has increased your vocabulary.

2. Begin your study of word roots with the first root on page 12. As you study the words, note that not every root of every word is analyzed but only those that will help you remember the word or that will later help you understand other words.

   The first definition is often a literal one (marked *lit.*) taken directly from the meaning of the roots. The definitions that follow are current ones, but usually only one or two definitions are given. For more, consult your dictionary.

3. Now do the exercises. If you write your answers in pencil, you can erase them if you want to try an exercise again. Answers are at the back of the book beginning on page 181.

4. Begin to keep a vocabulary journal, writing each day a few sentences about whatever interests you and using some of the words you have just learned. Putting the words into your own writing will help you remember them longer than if you merely fill in blanks. And from time to time you can reread your journal to review your words.

5. Finally, take the most important step in vocabulary building—use your newly learned words in conversation. Using a word in conversation will do more to help you remember it than any amount of silent study. USE A WORD THREE TIMES AND IT'S YOURS. Try using one new word a day. Begin at breakfast, and during the day find two more opportunities to use the word. Once you have used it three times, you'll be surprised how easily it will slip into your conversation.

And even if it's a word you don't expect to use, it will stay in your passive vocabulary so that you'll recognize it when you encounter it in your reading.

6. When you've finished studying the roots in the first part of the book, turn to the second part beginning on page 141, where additional roots are presented briefly. By studying this section you'll add still more words to your vocabulary and will discover more meaning in words you already know.

PRELIMINARY TEST   Test yourself on these words taken from college textbooks and current magazines. Check your answers with those on page 181.

b _____ 1. ambiguous   A.very large   B.having two possible meanings
C.seeking fame   D.exceptionally clear

d _____ 2. philanthropic   A.unmoved by criticism   B.fond of animals
C.sociable   D.charitable

a _____ 3. antipathy   A.strong dislike   B.worry   C.kindly feelings   D.ancient
times

a _____ 4. autonomy   A.the right of self-government   B. rule by a dictator
C.lack of government   D.rule by a few

d _____ 5. benefactor   A.one who receives money from a will   B.one who
receives a grant   C.distant relative   D.one who gives assistance

b _____ 6. anachronism   A.mistake in grammar   B.something out of its
proper historical time   C.incorrect calculation   D.clock for
navigation

a _____ 7. circumscribe   A.to overcome circumstances   B.to write an
autograph   C.to restrict the action of   D.to denounce

_____ 8. convivial   A.sociable   B.superficial   C.dangerous to life   D.vivid

b _____ 9. credulous   A.unbelieving   B.believing too readily   C.suspicious
D.having a good credit rating

c _____ 10. precursor   A.supervisor   B.beginner   C.forerunner   D.financial
officer

d _____ 11. pandemic   A.causing illness   B.causing a wild uproar
C.undemocratic   D.widespread

b _____ 12. euphemism   A.substitution of a pleasant for an unpleasant word
B.substitution of a specific term for a general one   C.false
statement   D.unrestrained praise

_____ 13. enervate   A.to weaken   B.to strengthen   C.to soothe   D.to excite

b _____ 14. epilogue   A.speech at a funeral   B.speech at the end of a play
C.speech at the beginning of a play   D.speech of apology

_____ 15. loquacious   A.full of life   B.having the ability to see through
things   C.understanding several languages   D.talkative

_____ 16. malinger   A.to move slowly   B.to spend too much time on details
C.to pretend to be ill to get out of work   D.to waste time

c _____ 17. missive   A.lost article   B.missing part   C.wrong answer   D.letter

b _____ 18. metamorphosis   A.life of a butterfly   B.change of form   C.mental
illness   D.abnormal growth

b _____ 19. panacea   A.remedy for all ills   B.folk remedy   C.widespread
epidemic   D.view from a mountain

_____ 20. apathy   A.dislike   B.strong interest   C.indifference   D.sympathy

_____ 21. impediment   A.lack of funds   B.hindrance   C.inability to speak
D.inability to walk

_____ 22. progeny   A.plan of action   B.gifted child   C.descendants
D.ancestors

_____ 23. assiduous   A.overbearing   B.haughty   C.critical   D.persevering

_____ 24. auspicious   A.unfavorable   B.favorable   C.foreboding evil
D.having doubts

_____ 25. subterranean   A.under cover   B.under the ocean   C.under the
earth   D.underhanded

_____ 26. supercilious   A.haughty   B.socially prominent   C.intellectually
superior   D.solicitous

_____ 27. syndrome   A.place where horse races are held   B.stadium
C.two adjoining domes   D.symptoms occurring together

WORD ROOTS IN ALPHABETICAL ORDER

A, AN—not, without

When A or AN meaning *not* or *without* comes at the beginning of certain words, it gives those words a negative meaning. Anything that is **asymmetric** is *not* symmetric, and anything that is **atypical** is *not* typical.

Atheist and **agnostic** both begin with the negative A and are close in meaning. An atheist [A without + THE god] is *without* a God whereas an agnostic [A not + GNOS to know] does *not* know whether there is a God. In other words, the atheist is sure there is no God whereas the agnostic simply does not know. If you are aware of the roots of these two words, you won't confuse their meanings.

Note how A or AN gives each of the following words a negative meaning.

atypical (ā tip' i kul)—not typical. *A classical concert performed by a rock group would certainly be atypical.*

asymmetrical (ā si met' ri kul) [A not + SYM together + METER measure]—*lit.* not measured together; not identical on both sides; not symmetrical. *She preferred asymmetrical flower arrangements.*

anonymous (uh non' uh mus) [AN without + ONYM name]—*lit.* without a name; having an unknown or unacknowledged name. *The donor of the new building wished to remain anonymous.*

anecdote (an' ik dōt) [AN not + EKDOTOS given out]—originally, not published (some stories were made public by publishing them, and others were kept private); now, merely a short account of some interesting or humorous incident. *The speaker enlivened his talk with humorous anecdotes.*

anarchy (an' ur kē) [AN without + ARCH ruler]—*lit.* without a ruler; political disorder and confusion. *The overthrow of the government resulted in anarchy.*

atheist (ā' thē ist) [A without + THE god]—*lit.* one who is without a God; one who denies the existence of God. *The atheist was unwilling to attend the church service.*

agnostic (ag nos' tik) [A not + GNOS to know]—one who does not know whether there is a God. *He had lost his former faith and had become an agnostic.*

amoral (ā mawr' ul)—neither moral nor immoral; without moral standards; unable to distinguish between right and wrong. *Infants are amoral.*

anomaly (uh nom' uh lē) [AN not + HOMO same]—*lit.* not the same (as others); a rare exception; something that is not normal. *Charles Darwin wrote, "There is no greater anomaly in nature than a bird that cannot fly."*

anesthetic (an is thet' ik) [AN without + ESTHET feeling]—a drug causing one to be insensitive to pain (without feeling). *Before the operation he was given an anesthetic.*

anemia (uh nē′ mē uh) [AN without + HEM blood]—*lit.* without blood; a deficiency of red corpuscles in the blood. *Her weakness was caused by anemia.*

ALSO: amorphous, analgesic, anodyne, apathetic, apathy, aphasia, atom (Consult the Word Index on page 193 for these words. Some are discussed under their other roots.)

EXERCISE 1 Write the appropriate A, AN word. Answers to the exercises will be found at the back of the book beginning on page 181.

1. The prisoner seemed to be without any standards, totally _____.

2. A dog that didn't like to chase rabbits would be an _____.

3. Formerly he was an _____, not knowing whether there is a God.

4. Now he calls himself an _____, denying the existence of God.

5. Larger on one side than on the other, the handmade pot was _____.

6. Her paper on Abraham Lincoln included many interesting _____.

7. She's usually so gracious that her leaving without even saying thank you

   was _____.

8. Either decreased production or increased destruction of red blood cells may

   cause _____.

9. After the riots, the country was in a state of _____.

EXERCISE 2 The best way to remember new words is to use them immediately in your writing and speaking. Therefore begin a vocabulary journal in which you write daily two or three sentences using some of your new words. If you write about things that interest you, then you'll be inclined to reread your journal occasionally as a review.

AMBI, AMPHI—around, both

In Roman times, candidates for public office, wearing white togas so that they could be easily seen, walked *around* (AMBI) talking to people and seeking votes. Before long, the term *ambitio* took on the meaning of bribery in seeking votes. But by the time the word came into English in the fourteenth century as **ambitious,** it had lost the idea of seeking votes or of bribery and meant merely "eager to succeed or to advance."

ambitious (am bish′ us)—originally, going around for votes; today, a strong desire to succeed. *She's ambitious and hopes to get a better job.*

amphitheater (am fuh thē′ uh tur)—an oval or round structure with tiers of seats around an open space. *The Drama Department presented Peer Gynt in the university amphitheater.*

ambiguous (am big′ yōō us) [AMBI around + AGERE to drive]—*lit.* to drive around (in an uncertain manner because there were few roads in early days); uncertain; having two possible meanings. *From her ambiguous answer, I couldn't tell whether she was complimenting or insulting me.*

ambiguity (am bi gyōō′ uh tē)—the quality of having two possible meanings. *The ambiguity in his writing leaves the reader puzzled.*

ambience (am′ bē uns)—the surrounding atmosphere. *The restaurant offered Old World ambience and charm along with modern efficiency.*

In the preceding words AMBI or AMPHI means *around.* In the following words it means *both.*

ambidextrous (am bi dek′ strus) [AMBI both + DEXTR right hand]—*lit.* both right hands; able to use both hands with equal ease. *Because she is ambidextrous, she plays a great game of tennis.*

amphibian (am fib′ ē un) [AMPHI both + BIO life]—an animal that lives both in the water and on land. *Frogs, toads, and salamanders are amphibians.* Also, an aircraft that can take off and land both on water and on land.

amphibious (am fib′ ē us) [AMPHI both + BIO life]—able to live or to travel both on land and in water. *The Marines went ashore in amphibious vehicles.*

ambivalent (am biv′ uh lunt)—having conflicting (both kinds of) feelings toward someone or something. *A child often feels ambivalent about a new baby in the family, both liking it and resenting it.*

ambivalence (am biv′ uh luns)—conflicting (both kinds of) feelings toward a person or thing. *The boy was experiencing ambivalence about giving his speech, wanting to give it and yet dreading it.*

EXERCISE 1 Write the appropriate AMBI, AMPHI word.

1. The senator's _____ replies left the audience unsure of his stand.

2. She felt _____ toward her baby brother, both loving him and hating him.

3. His _____ about the army made him undecided about re-enlisting.

4. The spicy aroma of Mideastern cuisine and the bright tapestries gave the restaurant an exotic _____ .

5. The _____ of that statement leaves it open to several interpretations.

6. The professor went to the lake to do some research on frogs and other _____ .

7. Since my son is _____, he can bat and pitch equally well with either hand.

8. Every seat in the _____ was filled for the political rally.

9. An _____ plant can grow either in water or on land.

Answers to the exercises will be found at the back of the book beginning on page 181.

EXERCISE 2 Write three sentences in your vocabulary journal using some of the AMBI, AMPHI words you have learned. Check with the sentence given in the explanation of each word to make sure you are using the word correctly. For example, *ambiguous* is an adjective whereas *ambiguity* is a noun. But even without thinking about parts of speech, you'll use the words correctly if you follow the model sentences.

ANN, ENN—year

Words containing ANN or ENN will have something to do with *year*. An **anniversary** is the return of some event every *year*. An **annuity** is a fund that pays a person money every *year*. **Annual** means happening every *year*, and **semiannual** means happening every half *year*. **Biannual** and **biennial** are easily confused because they both come from BI *two* and ANN or ENN *year*. One just has to remember that biannual (like semiannual) means occurring two times a *year* and that biennial means occurring every two *years*.

annual—yearly

anniversary [ANN year + VERS to turn]—the yearly return of the date of some memorable event

semiannual [SEMI half + ANN year]—half yearly; occurring two times a year

biannual (bī an' yōo ul) [BI two + ANN year]—occurring two times a year. *The treasurer made biannual (or semiannual) reports in January and July.*

biennial (bī en' ē ul) [BI two + ENN year]—occurring every two years. *The society holds a biennial convention in the odd-numbered years.*

centennial (sen ten' ē ul) [CENT hundred + ENN year]—a 100th anniversary. *The Exposition in Montreal in 1967 celebrated the centennial of Canadian Confederation.*

perennial (puh ren' ē ul) [PER through + ENN year]—having a life cycle lasting through more than two years, as a perennial plant. *In his garden he planted only perennials so that he wouldn't have to replant every year.* Also, lasting many years, as perennial youth. *She was a perennial student, still taking courses after she was 50.*

per annum (pur an' um) [PER through + ANN year]—by the year; annually. *The chairperson received a fixed salary per annum.*

annals (an'uls)—a written account of events year by year; historical records. *We searched the annals of the medical society to find when the vaccine had first been tested.*

annuity (uh nōo' uh tē)—an investment that provides fixed payments yearly or at other regular intervals. *After paying into his annuity for years, he now receives a check each month.*

millennium (muh len' ē um) [MILLI thousand + ENN year]—a period of a thousand years; specifically, the thousand years when, according to the New Testament, Christ will return to rule the world; thus, a period of happiness and prosperity. *Some reformers today are hoping for nothing short of a millennium.*

superannuated (soo pur an' yoo ā tid) [SUPER above + ANN year]—*lit.* beyond the year of retirement; retired because of age. *Now that he was superannuated, he had time for his hobbies.*

ALSO: Anno Domini (abbrev. AD), bicentennial, triennial

EXERCISE 1 What word containing ANN or ENN names the following?

1. a 100th anniversary _____

2. a period of great happiness and prosperity _____

3. a written account of events year by year _____

4. an investment providing payments yearly or at other intervals _____

5. the yearly return of the date of a memorable event _____

What word containing ANN or ENN describes the following?

6. something happening twice a year _____ or _____

7. something happening every two years _____

8. something lasting through many years _____

9. a person retired because of age _____

EXERCISE 2 REVIEW Fill in the blanks with words from the last three sections.

1. The vivid yellows and reds in the room created an _____ of warmth and vitality.
2. The lecturer did not make his point clear and left the audience puzzled by

   his _____.
3. I assure you that I don't usually miss appointments; my missing that one

   was definitely _____.

4. After she was _____, she still wanted to work and took another job.
5. I'm feeling _____ about volunteering for that job. I know I should do it, but I really don't want to.

ANTE, ANTI—before

ANTE, ANTI meaning *before* must not be confused with ANTI meaning *against* (p. 22). The ANTE spelling always means *before*—either *before* in space or *before* in time. **Anteroom** and **anterior** are *before* in space whereas **ante**, **antedate**, and **antebellum** are *before* in time.

Another before-in-time word is **antediluvian**. Originally it meant *before the Flood* described in the Bible story of Noah and the Ark. In fact its two roots say exactly that [ANTE before + DILUVIUM flood], but today it has come to mean merely very old or primitive. Whenever you want to exaggerate the age of something, you can call it antediluvian. Young people may think their elders' ideas are antediluvian. A farmer without a tractor or a large office without a computer might be described as using antediluvian methods. And if you are trying to convince someone—or yourself—that your car is old enough to be turned in on a new model, you might refer to it as antediluvian.

anteroom (an' ti room)—a room before the main room; a waiting room. *In the director's anteroom were a dozen actors waiting to try out for the part.*

anterior (an tir' ē ur)—located before or in front (as opposed to posterior, located behind). *The anterior legs of the kangaroo are shorter than the posterior ones.*

antecedent (an tuh sēd' unt) [ANTE before + CED to go]—anything that logically goes before something else. *Cricket was the antecedent of baseball.* Also, the word, phrase, or clause to which a pronoun refers. *In the sentence "Every boy was in his place," boy is the antecedent of the pronoun his.*

ante (an' tē)—the amount each poker player must put into the pot before receiving his cards. *Feeling confident, he upped the ante.*

antedate (an' ti dāt)—to occur before something else. *The Revolutionary War antedates the Civil War.*

antebellum (an tē bel' um) [ANTE before + BELL war]—before the war, especially before the Civil War. *The novel Gone with the Wind begins in the South in antebellum days.*

antediluvian (an ti di loo' vē un) [ANTE before + DILUVIUM flood]—before the Flood described in the Bible; old-fashioned or primitive. *Compared with the cars my friends drive, mine is antediluvian.*

ante meridiem (an tē muh rid' ē um) (abbreviated AM) [ANTE before + MERIDI noon]—before noon. *I have an appointment at 10 AM.*

A variant spelling—ANTI—also means before-in-time in the following words.

anticipate (an tis′ uh pāt) [ANTI before + CAP to take]—*lit.* to take before; to realize beforehand. *No one anticipated such an outcome.*

antique (an tēk′)—belonging to an earlier (before) period. *In the parade were a dozen antique automobiles.*

✓ **antiquated** (an′ tuh kwā tid)—so old as to be no longer useful. *The factory had to replace the antiquated machinery.*

antiquity (an tik′ wuh tē)—ancient (before) times. *The museum specializes in jewelry from antiquity.*

antiquarian (an ti kwer′ ē un)—a dealer in old (before) rare books. *The antiquarian appraised the rare first edition.*

EXERCISE 1 Write the appropriate ANTE, ANTI word.

1. The office manager discarded some _____ typewriters.
2. She thought her parents' rules so hopelessly old-fashioned that she called

   them _____.
3. A grasshopper's wings are attached to the _____ part of its body.
4. Trees with hanging Spanish moss surrounded the old Southern mansion of

   the _____ period.
5. We found an _____ who was willing to buy the battered old copy of *Walden*.
6. In the museum were various artifacts from _____.

7. The landing of the Norsemen on this continent is said to _____ the landing of Columbus.
8. A pronoun should agree with the noun that is its _____.

9. I dropped out of the poker game because the _____ was too high.

EXERCISE 2 Write three sentences in your journal using some of the ANTE, ANTI words.

ANTHROP—human

Knowing that ANTHROP means *human* clarifies the meaning of several long words. **Anthropology** [ANTHROP human + -LOGY study of] is a study of the development and behavior of *human* beings. A **philanthropist** [PHIL to love + ANTHROP human] loves *human* beings and promotes *human* welfare by charitable acts or gifts. A **misanthrope** [MIS to hate + ANTHROP human], on the other hand, hates *human* beings.

anthropology (an thruh pol′ uh jē) [ANTHROP human + -LOGY study of]—a study of the physical, social, and cultural development and behavior of human beings. *The anthropology class was discussing the fact that Eskimos have many different words for snow.*

anthropologist (an thruh pol′ uh jist) [ANTHROP human + -LOGY study of]—one who studies the physical, social, and cultural development and behavior of human beings. *The anthropologist Margaret Mead lived with a primitive tribe in Samoa to study their culture.*

philanthropist (fi lan′ thruh pist) [PHIL to love + ANTHROP human]—one who loves people, particularly one who gives money to benefit humanity. *Andrew Carnegie, a famous philanthropist, gave money to build public libraries.*

philanthropy (fi lan′ thruh pē) [PHIL to love + ANTHROP human]—the effort to increase the well-being of humanity by charitable donations. *The corporation was known for its philanthropy as well as for its good business practices.*

philanthropic (fil un throp′ ik) [PHIL to love + ANTHROP human]—charitable. *The United Fund aids many philanthropic organizations.*

misanthrope (mis′ un thrōp) [MIS to hate + ANTHROP human)—one who hates people. *Only a misanthrope would have such a low opinion of the human race.*

misanthropic (mis un throp′ ik) [MIS to hate + ANTHROP human]—characterized by hatred or scorn for people. *Ebenezer Scrooge shows his misanthropic attitude when he replies to a Merry Christmas greeting with "Bah! Humbug!"*

anthropoid (an′ thruh poid) [ANTHROP human + OID resembling]—resembling humans. *Gorillas, chimpanzees, orangutans, and gibbons are anthropoid apes.*

anthropomorphism (an thruh pō mawr′ fiz um) [ANTHROP human + MORPH form]—the attributing of human form or characteristics to a god, animal, or inanimate thing. *Anthropomorphism is a part of many primitive cultures, with rivers, trees, and animals being given human characteristics.*

anthropomorphic (an thruh pō mawr′ fik) [ANTHROP human + MORPH form]—thought of as having human form or characteristics. *The ani-*

mal *characters in Beatrix Potter's* Peter Rabbit *are anthropomorphic, speaking and acting like humans.*

anthropocentric (an thruh pō sen′ trik) [ANTHROP human + CENTR center]—considering human beings to be the center and purpose of the universe. *Early societies thought that the universe was anthropocentric and that the sun, moon, and stars were created for human benefit.*

EXERCISE 1 Write the appropriate ANTHROP word.

1. The Uncle Remus stories about Br'er Rabbit have _____ characters.

2. I heard a lecture on the culture of the Amazon by a famous _____.

3. His hateful attitude toward his neighbors branded him as a _____.

4. With our expanding view of the universe, we can no longer think of it as

   _____.

5. Sign language can be taught to an _____ ape such as the chimpanzee.

6. The college is hoping that some _____ will donate a large sum to its endowment fund.

EXERCISE 2 List at least three stories or cartoons that have anthropomorphic characters.

EXERCISE 3 In your vocabulary journal write some sentences using ANTHROP words.

ANTI—against, opposite

ANTI meaning *against* is easy to spot in such words as **antifreeze, antitrust,** and **antisocial,** but it can also help clarify more difficult words.

A couple of ANTI words, which you probably won't have occasion to use and which won't be included in any of the tests in this book, are interesting just because of their stories.

Antipodes (an tip' uh dēz) [ANTI opposite + POD foot] means literally "with the feet opposite" and refers to any place on the *opposite* side of the earth since the people there seem to be standing upside down with their feet *opposite* to ours. The British refer to Australia and New Zealand as the Antipodes because those countries are on the *opposite* side of the earth.

Another word with an unusual history is **antimacassar** (an tē muh kas' ur). In the nineteenth century, men used macassar oil, imported from Macassar, Indonesia, as a hair dressing, and they often left grease spots on the backs of upholstered chairs where they rested their heads. Their wives, therefore, crocheted small covers to put on the backs of the chairs to keep the macassar oil from soiling the upholstery. The covers were called antimacassars (ANTI against + MACASSAR macassar oil). Gradually all covers protecting the backs and arms of upholstered furniture came to be called antimacassars.

antibiotic (an ti bī ot' ik) [ANTI against + BIO life]—a substance produced by a microorganism that destroys other harmful (living) microorganisms. *Penicillin is an antibiotic.*

antiseptic (an tuh sep' tik) [ANTI against + SEPT putrid]—against infection; capable of destroying microorganisms that cause disease. *The nurse washed the wound with an antiseptic solution.*

antidote (an' ti dōt) [ANTI against + DOT to give]—a medicine that counteracts (works against) poison or disease. *After the snake bit him, he was quickly given an antidote.* Also, something that prevents injurious effects. *Plentiful jobs are one of the best antidotes to crime.* Also, something that relieves or counteracts. *The comedy was a pleasant antidote to all the tragedies we had seen.*

antagonist (an tag' uh nist) [ANTI against + AGON struggle]—a person one struggles against in a contest. *The young wrestler was stronger than his antagonist.*

antiphonal (an tif' uh nul) [ANTI against + PHON sound]—*lit.* one sound against another; sung in alternation, one voice responding to another. *The choir sang an antiphonal psalm, with the sopranos responding to each line sung by the basses.*

In the preceding words ANTI means *against*; in the following words it means *opposite*.

anticlimax (an ti klī′ maks)—*lit.* the opposite of the climax; a sudden drop from the important to the commonplace. *Her present uninteresting job is an anticlimax to a brilliant career.*

Antarctica (ant ark′ ti kuh)—the continent opposite the Arctic. *The Arctic is the region at the North Pole; Antarctica is the continent opposite it at the South Pole.*

antithesis (an tith′ uh sis) [ANTI opposite + THES to place]—*lit.* one idea placed opposite another; the exact opposite. *Love is the antithesis of hate.* Also, ideas contrasted in balanced phrases, as *"To err is human; to forgive, divine."*

ALSO: antacid, antagonize, antihero, antipathy, antitoxin, antonym
(Consult the Word Index on page 193 for these words. Some are discussed under their other roots.)

EXERCISE 1   Write the appropriate ANTI word.

1. Coming at the end of a stimulating program, his dull speech was an

   _____.

2. The man who challenged him to fight was a powerful _____.
3. He wanted luxury; she wanted a simple life. Thus his goals were the

   _____ of hers.
4. Diseases that were once fatal can now be cured with _____.

5. The _____ response of the men's voices in the choir loft at the back of the church to the women's voices at the front was effective.
6. The continent of _____ surrounds the South Pole.

7. Having an interesting hobby is an _____ to boredom.

EXERCISE 2   In your vocabulary journal write some sentences using ANTI words.

AUTO—self

AUTO, meaning *self*, was a common Greek root, but it took on added meaning in America in the late nineteenth century when it was applied to the new vehicle that could "move by itself"—the **automobile** [AUTO self + MOB to move].

automobile [AUTO self + MOB to move]—*lit.* a self-moving vehicle

autopsy [AUTO self + OP sight]—*lit.* a seeing for onself; an examination of a dead body to discover the cause of death

automat [AUTO self + MAT to act]—*lit.* a self-acting machine; a once-popular type of restaurant in which food was delivered to patrons from coin-operated compartments

automatic [AUTO self + MAT to act]—operating by itself

automation [AUTO self + MAT to act]—a system using self-operating machines

automaton (aw tom' uh tun) [AUTO self + MAT to act]—an apparatus that functions by itself; a robot. Also, a person who has lost all human qualities and acts mechanically. *Because she had been performing the same task on the assembly line for so long, she felt like an automaton.*

autocrat (aw' tuh krat) [AUTO self + CRAT to rule]—an absolute ruler; a domineering, self-willed person. *When the autocrat took over the country, the people lost all their power.*

autocracy (aw tok' ruh sē) [AUTO self + CRAC to rule]—government by a single person. *The country had become an autocracy and was ripe for revolt.*

autocratic (aw tuh krat' ik) [AUTO self + CRAT to rule]—*lit.* ruling by oneself; domineering. *The supervisor was autocratic, accepting suggestions from no one.*

autonomy (aw ton' uh mē) [AUTO self + NOM law)—the right of self-government. *Many small nations are struggling for autonomy.*

autonomous (aw ton' uh mus) [AUTO self + NOM law]—self-governing. *Released from state control, the college finally became autonomous.*

autonomic (aw tuh nom' ik) [AUTO self + NOM law]—pertaining to the autonomic nervous system, which acts according to its own (self) laws rather than through voluntary control and regulates the heart, digestive system, and so forth. *He was trying to learn to control the actions of his autonomic nervous system through biofeedback.*

ALSO: autobiography, autograph

EXERCISE 1 Write the appropriate AUTO word.

1. He was _____ in his control of the company, allowing his subordinates to have no power.
2. With her mind on more important matters, she performed her household

   tasks like an _____.
3. The people were tired of being ruled by an _____ and of having no say in their government.
4. They were threatening to revolt in the hope of changing their _____ to a democracy.
5. The digestion of food is controlled by the _____ nervous system.

EXERCISE 2 REVIEW Write C in front of each sentence in which all words are used correctly.

_____ 1. Antiphonal means one voice singing in response to another.

_____ 2. An anonymous note is a threatening note.

_____ 3. An annuity provides fixed payments at regular intervals.

_____ 4. An anthropoid animal resembles human beings.

_____ 5. An antecedent is something that goes before something else.

_____ 6. He and his antagonist put up a good fight against the other tennis team.

_____ 7. Ambivalence means having two conflicting emotions at the same time.

_____ 8. An agnostic does not believe in God.

_____ 9. The Vietnam War antedates World War II.

_____ 10. Antediluvian means old-fashioned.

_____ 11. Something asymmetrical has both sides exactly alike.

_____ 12. The leader of the commune is asking for a millennium.

_____ 13. Biannual means occurring two times a year.

_____ 14. Daily walks are an antidote to tension.

_____ 15. Traveling through Antarctica, the explorer finally reached the North Pole.

_____ 16. A biennial meeting is one that is held every two years.

_____ 17. The annals of a society are its yearly records.

_____ 18. Antiquity means ancient times.

_____ 19. The antithesis is the main idea of an essay.

_____ 20. A bird without feathers would be an anomaly.

BENE—well, good

Words that begin with BENE always describe something *good*—an action, a result, or an attitude.

benefit [BENE well + FAC to do]—anything that promotes well being; a payment to one in need

beneficial [BENE well + FAC to do]—producing benefits; advantageous

benediction [BENE well + DICT to speak]—the calling for divine blessing, usually at the end of a religious service

benevolent (buh nev' uh lunt) [BENE well + VOL to wish]—*lit.* wishing someone well; inclined to do good. *The supervisor had a benevolent attitude toward her staff, giving them bonuses and days off.*

benign (bi nīn')—having a kindly (good) attitude or disposition. *The parents looked upon the capers of their son with benign tolerance.* Also, in medicine, mild in character; not malignant. *The growth proved to be benign rather than malignant.*

(Benevolent and benign are close synonyms. Both mean having a kindly attitude, but benevolent often includes the idea of doing something charitable. And benign has a medical meaning opposite to malignant.)

benevolence (buh nev' uh luns) [BENE well + VOL to wish]—an inclination to do good; a kindly or charitable act. *The benevolence of the church members was shown by their generous contributions to charity.*

beneficence (buh nef' uh suns) [BENE good + FAC to do]—*lit.* the doing of good; kindness; charity. *The scholarships were funded through the beneficence of the alumni.*

(Benevolence and beneficence are close synonyms.)

benefactor (ben uh fak' tur) [BENE good + FAC to do]—*lit.* one who does something good; one who gives help or financial assistance. *The college owed much to its generous benefactors.*

beneficiary (ben uh fish' ē er ē) [BENE good + FAC to do]—a person who receives benefits, as from a will or an insurance policy. *He was the beneficiary of his father's will.*

ALSO: beneficent

EXERCISE 1 Write the appropriate BENE word.

1. The congregation rose for the final _____.

2. A _____ of the university provided funds for medical research.

3. The firm was saved from bankruptcy by the _____ of a group of employees.

4. Fortunately they found that the tumor was _____.

5. This country has a _____ attitude toward developing nations, often giving them financial aid.

6. She was the _____ of her father's insurance policy.

7. The displaced families were provided for by the _____ of several charitable organizations.

EXERCISE 2 REVIEW Write C in front of each sentence in which all words are used correctly.

___C___ 1. They watched the monkeys and other amphibians at the zoo.

___C___ 2. When the children knocked at his door, the old misanthrope shouted for them to go away.

___C___ 3. Instruments today can measure the functioning of the autonomic nervous system.

___C___ 4. She received a stated salary per annum plus some bonuses.

_____ 5. Anthropomorphic beliefs put humans at the center of the universe.

___C___ 6. Giving no thought to her job, she worked like an automaton.

___C___ 7. An autopsy was necessary to determine the cause of death.

___C___ 8. After being a colony for years, the island finally achieved autonomy.

___C___ 9. Through the philanthropy of a large corporation, a day-care center was established.

___C___ 10. The anthropology class was studying a Northwest Indian culture.

___C___ 11. Prosperity is an antidote for political unrest.

EXERCISE 3 In your journal write some sentences using BENE words.

BI—two

Back in the days of sailing ships, according to one story, the bread taken along on the voyages always became moldy. Then someone discovered that by baking the bread *twice*, enough moisture could be removed so that it remained edible during long voyages. The new kind of bread was called **biscuit** [BI two + COQUERE to cook] or *twice*-baked bread. Today biscuits are no longer twice-baked but are merely quick breads or non-yeast breads baked in small cakes.

biscuit [BI two + COQUERE to cook]—*lit.* twice-cooked or baked; a quick bread baked in small pieces

bisect [BI two + SECT to cut]—to cut in two, as a diameter bisects a circle

biceps [BI two + CAPIT head]—any muscle having two heads or points of origin, as the large muscle at the front of the upper arm

bicentennial [BI two + CENT hundred + ENN year]—a 200th anniversary, as the United States bicentennial in 1976

binoculars [BI two + OCUL eye]—field glasses for use with two eyes (in contrast to the telescope, which is for use with one eye only)

bigamy (big′ uh mē) [BI two + GAM marriage]—marrying one person while legally married to another. *Bigamy is against the law in this country.*

biped (bī′ ped) [BI two + PED foot]—a two-footed animal. *Humans are the only bipeds who laugh.*

bivalve (bī′ valv)—a mollusk having two valves or shells hinged together, as a mussel or clam. *The oyster is a bivalve valued by both gourmets and jewelers.*

bicuspid (bī kus′ pid) [BI two + CUSPID point]—a tooth having two points. *A human adult has eight bicuspids.*

bilateral (bī lat′ ur ul) [BI two + LATER side]—having or involving two sides; binding on both parties (in contrast to unilateral in which only one party has an obligation). *According to a bilateral agreement, each of the two nations will cut armament expenditures.*

bilingual (bī ling′ gwul) [BI two + LINGU language]—able to use two languages. *In Canada job opportunities are greater for a bilingual person.*

bipartisan (bī pahr′ tuh zun)—consisting of or supported by two parties, especially two major political parties. *Assured of bipartisan support, the senator was confident the bill would pass.*

bicameral (bī kam′ ur ul) [BI two + CAMER chamber]—composed of two legislative chambers or branches. *The United States has a bicameral legislative system composed of the Senate and the House of Representatives.*

binary (bĭ′ nuh rē)—composed of two different parts. *A binary star consists of two stars revolving around a common center of mass and often appearing as a single star.* Also, a number system in which the base used is two. *Computers use the binary counting system, which has just two values: 1 and 0.*

ALSO: biannual, bicycle, biennial, bifocal, bigamist, binomial, bipartite

---

EXERCISE 1 Write the appropriate BI word.

1. The two nations signed a _____ trade agreement.

2. The committee was _____, composed of representatives from both political parties.

3. Laws must be passed by both houses in our _____ system.

4. The pinkish angel wing shells are the attractive outer covering of a

   _____.

5. The new highway will _____ the city, bringing more business to downtown stores.

6. Raising his arm, he flexed his strong _____.

7. With her _____ she was able to get an excellent view of the races.

8. A _____ celebration occurs every 200 years.

9. She is _____, speaking both English and French fluently.

10. When it was discovered that he had two wives at the same time, a charge

    of _____ was brought against him.

11. A tooth ending in two points is called a _____.

12. Any animal that walks on two feet is called a _____.

13. A _____ star is really two stars orbiting around a common mass.

EXERCISE 2 In your vocabulary journal write three sentences using some of the BI words.

BIO—life

The root BIO meaning *life* combines with SYM meaning *together* to form an interesting word—**symbiosis,** the living together of two dissimilar organisms, usually for the benefit of both. For example, the hermit crab lives among the petal-like but lethal tentacles of the sea anemone and is protected from its enemies by the stinging power of the tentacles. The anemone, on the other hand, is carried in the claws or on the back of the hermit crab to new feeding grounds. Thus the symbiosis is beneficial to both.

biology [BIO life + -LOGY study of]—the study of plant and animal life
biochemistry—chemistry relating to living organisms
biography [BIO life + GRAPH to write]—a written account of someone's life
autobiography [AUTO self + BIO life + GRAPH to write]—an account of a person's life written by that person

biodegradable (bī ō di grā′ duh bul)—capable of being broken down by microorganisms and absorbed by the environment. *She switched to a biodegradable detergent, which would not pollute the streams.*
biofeedback (bī ō fēd′ bak)—a technique for consciously regulating a bodily (life) function thought to be involuntary, as heartbeat or blood pressure, by using an instrument to monitor the function and to signal changes in it. *She found that she could slow her pulse by using biofeedback.*
biopsy (bī′ op sē) [BIO life + OP sight]—*lit.* a seeing of live tissues; the examination of tissues removed from the living body. *The biopsy revealed that the growth was benign.*
biosphere (bī′ uh sfir)—the part of the earth, extending from its crust out into the surrounding atmosphere, in which living things exist. *Many parts of the biosphere remain to be explored.*
symbiosis (sim bi ō′ sis) [SYM together + BIO life]—the living together of two dissimilar organisms, often to their mutual benefit. *The symbiosis of algae and fungi forms lichens.*
symbiotic (sim bi ot′ ik) [SYM together + BIO life]—living together in a close relationship, often to the benefit of both. *In a symbiotic relationship, ants protect defenseless aphids and then "milk" them for their honeydew.*

ALSO: amphibian, antibiotic, bionic, microbe

30

EXERCISE 1 Write the appropriate BIO word.

1. Parts of the earth's _____ are inhabited only by micro-organisms.

2. The _____ relationship of ants and aphids is beneficial to both.

3. The relationship of the ants and aphids is an example of _____.

4. To discover the type of tumor, the doctor performed a _____.

5. The attempt to control involuntary bodily functions is called _____.

6. Many people are refusing to buy egg cartons that are not _____.

EXERCISE 2 REVIEW Write C in front of each sentence in which all words are used correctly.

_____ 1. The manager was autocratic, allowing no one else to share his power.

_____ 2. Through the beneficence of the alumni, the college was able to offer ten scholarships.

_____ 3. The bilingual professor could speak four languages.

_____ 4. The wrestler flexed his biceps in preparation for the match.

_____ 5. My teenage brother is an anomaly; he doesn't like video games.

_____ 6. As one of the benefactors of the will, she received a thousand dollars.

_____ 7. A biped is a two-wheeled vehicle.

_____ 8. A child's first front tooth is a bicuspid.

EXERCISE 3 REVIEW On one of the blank pages at the end of this book, start a WORD LIST of words you hope to use in the future. Keeping a word list is an excellent way to increase your vocabulary because rereading your list occasionally will bring to mind words you might otherwise forget.

CHRON—time

Like all other CHRON words, **anachronism** has something to do with *time*. It's the term applied to anything that is out of its proper historical *time*. For example, it would be an anachronism to mention antibiotics in writing about the nineteenth century.

Shakespeare let several anchronisms slip into his plays. He speaks of a clock striking in *Julius Caesar*, but striking clocks had not been invented at the time of Julius Caesar. And in *King John* he mentions using cannons, but the scenes in that play took place many years before cannons were used in England.

chronic (kron′ ik)—continuing for a long time, as a chronic disease. *A chronic complainer, he was never happy with his situation.*

chronicle (kron′ i kul)—an account of events arranged in order of time. The Anglo-Saxon Chronicle *gives an account of twelve centuries of British history.*

chronology (kruh nol′ uh jē) [CHRON time + -LOGY study of]—a list of events arranged according to time of occurrence. *He had memorized the chronology of the reigns of the English monarchs.*

chronological (kron uh loj′ i kul)—arranged in order of time of occurrence. *The play dramatizes in chronological order the events that led to the bombing of Pearl Harbor.*

chronometer (kruh nom′ uh tur) [CHRON time + METER measure]—an instrument for measuring time precisely, especially in navigation. *Before making an entry in the log, the captain consulted the chronometer.*

synchronize (sin′ kruh nīz) [SYN together + CHRON time)—to cause to operate (keep time) in unison, as to synchronize watches or to synchronize the sound with the film in a motion picture. *The sound track of the film was not synchronized with the picture.*

anachronism (uh nak′ ruh niz um) [ANA back + CHRON time]—anything out of its proper historical time. *To include an electric typewriter in a story set in 1920 would be an anachronism.*

EXERCISE 1 Write the appropriate CHRON word.

1. We made a _____ list of the trips we had taken during the last three years.
2. Pedal cars are an _____ in *The Flintstones*, a cartoon series set in the Stone Age.

3. Let's _____ our watches so that we can meet for lunch at twelve.

4. The _____ is only one of many precision instruments on a ship.
5. For ten years he has worked on the assembly line, and for ten years he has suffered from _____ boredom.

EXERCISE 2 REVIEW Underline the appropriate word.

1. We listened patiently to a (chronicle, chronometer) of all her ills.
2. The absence of government is called (autocracy, anarchy).
3. In a (bilateral, bicameral) system of government, one legislative body acts as a check on the other.
4. The college was the (benefactor, beneficiary) of a government grant.
5. The museum in Atlanta was in an old mansion of (antiquarian, antebellum) days.
6. It would be an (ambiguity, anachronism) to describe walking on the moon in a story set in 1950.
7. His (beneficent, misanthropic) attitude toward his fellow workers made him disliked by everyone.
8. It was once common to believe in an (anthropocentric, anthropomorphic) universe, with everything created for the benefit of humans.
9. After a long struggle, the small country finally became (autonomous, autocratic).
10. The (autopsy, biopsy) shows that the growth at present is not malignant.
11. The class was learning to control autonomic functions through (biopsy, biofeedback).
12. They decided to spend their savings on some beautiful (antiquated, antique) furniture.
13. The manager of the hotel tried to create an (ambivalence, ambience) of luxury.

EXERCISE 3 In your journal write some sentences with CHRON words.

CIRCUM—around

CIRCUM always means *around*. A **circumference** is the boundary line *around* a circle. To **circumnavigate** the globe is to go *around* it. A **circumstance** [CIRCUM around + STA to stand] is literally something standing *around*. Perhaps the circumstance that is standing *around* and keeping you from going to a movie is a lack of money.

circumference [CIRCUM around + FER to carry]—*lit.* a line carried around; the boundary line of a circle

circumnavigate [CIRCUM around + NAV to sail]—to sail around

circumstance [CIRCUM around + STA to stand]—*lit.* something standing around; a fact or event accompanying another fact or event

circumvent (sur kum vent') [CIRCUM around + VEN to come]—*lit.* to come around; to get around or to overcome by artful maneuvering. *By offering a small wage increase, the management hoped to circumvent a walkout.*

circumspect (sur' kum spekt) [CIRCUM around + SPEC to look]—looking around carefully; cautious. *He had learned to be circumspect in offering suggestions to his temperamental boss.*

circumscribe (sur' kum skrīb) [CIRCUM around + SCRIB to write]—*lit.* to write a line around the bounds; to limit; to confine. *The rules of the private school circumscribed the daily activities of the students.*

circumlocution (sur kum lō kyoo' shun) [CIRCUM around + LOC to speak]—a roundabout way of saying something. *Saying "A number of other commitments will make it impossible for me to find the time to attend the meeting" would be a circumlocution for the simple statement "I can't attend the meeting."*

circuit (sur' kit)—the regular journey around a territory by a person performing duties. *The newspaper boy made his usual circuit.* Also, a closed path followed by an electric current. *When the circuit was interrupted, the lights went out.* Also, an arrangement of electrically or electromagnetically connected components. *Computers use integrated circuits.*

circuitous (sur kyoo' uh tus)—roundabout; winding. *Because she didn't know the way, she took us by a rather circuitous route. His speech was full of circuitous arguments that got nowhere.*

EXERCISE 1 Write the appropriate CIRCUM word.

1. "He does not exhibit the self-control appropriate to his age" is simply a

   _____ for "He's a brat."
2. He opposed the plan and did all he could to _____ it.

3. Because she didn't want to offend anyone, she was always _____
   about offering advice.
4. Don't let all the rules _____ your creativity.

5. We followed a _____ path up the mountain.

6. Philippe Jeantot set a world record when he _____ the
   globe solo in his sailboat in 159 days in 1983.

EXERCISE 2 Turn the following circumlocution into a concise statement.
   With reference to your letter, I wish to inform you that we have taken your
complaint under consideration and have come to the conclusion that the TV
set that you purchased from our company should be repaired by us free of
charge.

_____

_____

EXERCISE 3 REVIEW Write C in front of each sentence in which all the
words are used correctly.

_____ 1. She gave us a chronological account of her visit to the oral surgeon.

_____ 2. Pollution is causing changes in parts of the biosphere.

_____ 3. The Nuclear Waste Policy Act of 1982 passed with bipartisan support.

_____ 4. Plastic containers, which are not biodegradable, are cluttering the
   countryside.

_____ 5. After synchronizing our watches, we agreed to meet at the theater
   at seven.

_____ 6. She became worried when the doctor found that the tumor was
   benign.

_____ 7. A bicentennial celebration was held at the end of 100 years.

_____ 8. To bisect an apple is to cut it in four pieces.

COM, CON, COL, COR—together, with

Companion takes on new meaning when we learn its roots. A companion [COM with + PAN bread] was originally a person one shared one's bread *with*. We don't think of that original meaning today, and yet when we want to be hospitable, we invite our companions to share our food.

COM meaning *together* or *with* is sometimes difficult to spot because it so often changes its last letter to be like the first letter of the root following it. Thus COMloquial becomes COLloquial, COMnect becomes CONnect, and COMrelate becomes CORrelate. Sometimes the letter *m* is dropped completely, and COMeducation becomes COeducation. Changing the last letter in these ways makes the pronunciation easier. On page 6 is a further discussion of changes in root spelling.

Sometimes, as in **condone** and **compunction,** COM is used merely as an intensive, giving more emphasis to the root that follows.

compress—to press together

complicate [COM together + PLIC to fold]—*lit.* to fold together; to make intricate or involved

computer [COM together + PUTARE to reckon]—an electronic machine that performs high-speed mathematical and logical calculations when given coded information

commotion [COM together + MOT to move]—people moving together; social disorder

committee [COM together + MIT to send]—a group of people sent together to consider some matter

companion [COM with + PAN bread]—*lit.* a person one shares one's bread with; a comrade

composition [COM together + POS to put]—a putting together of parts to form a whole

contemporary [CON together + TEMPOR time]—*lit.* together in time; belonging to the same age

convention [CON together + VEN to come]—the coming together of the members of a group

cooperate—to operate together

coexist—to exist together

coeducation—education of men and women together

collaborate (kuh lab′ uh rāt)—to labor together. *Two committee members are collaborating in preparing the report.*

correlate (kor' uh lāt)—to relate together; to show relationship. *The accountant is trying to correlate this year's figures with last year's.*

convene (kun vēn') [CON together + VEN to come]—to come together formally. *The committee will convene next week.*

condone (kun dōn') [COM (intensive) + DON to give]—to forgive or overlook (an offense). *The public can't condone the dishonest dealings of the company representative.*

coherent (kō hir' unt) [CO together + HER to stick]—*lit.* sticking together; logically consistent; having an orderly relation of parts. *The lecture, with its rambling stories, was not very coherent.*

consensus (kun sen' sus) [CON together + SENS to feel]—*lit.* a feeling together; general agreement. *No consensus has been reached about the safety of nuclear plants.*

condominium (kahn duh min' ē uhm) [CON together + DOMINIUM ownership]—a building in which the living units are owned individually and the grounds are owned together. *Because they didn't want to take care of a yard, they bought a condominium instead of a house.*

commiserate (kuh miz' uh rāt) [COM with + MISER wretched, pitiable]—*lit.* to feel wretched with someone; to sympathize. *She commiserated with me over the loss of my job.*

congenital (kun jen' uh tul) [CON together + GEN birth]—*lit.* born together; existing at birth. *The child has a congenital heart defect.*

convivial (kun viv' ē ul) [CON together + VIV to live]—fond of eating, drinking, and being sociable together. *In a convivial mood, the guests stayed until midnight.*

commodious (kuh mō' dē us) [COM with + MOD measure]—with plenty of room; spacious. *Their mobile home was more commodious than I had anticipated.*

commensurate (kuh men' suh rit) [COM together + MENS to measure]—*lit.* measured together; equal in measure or size; proportionate. *The pay should be commensurate with the work.*

collusion (kuh loo' zhun) [COL together + LUD to play]—*lit.* playing together; a secret agreement between two or more persons for a deceitful purpose. *The manager suspected collusion between the two employees.*

compunction (kum pungk' shun) [COM (intensive) + PUNCT to prick]—*lit.* a prick of conscience; an uneasiness caused by a sense of guilt; a slight regret; a twinge of misgiving about an anticipated action. *He felt some compunction about taking so much of the tutor's time.*

consummate (kun sum' it) [CON together + SUMMA sum]—*lit.* summed up together; complete or perfect in every respect; supremely accomplished or skilled. *She was a consummate artist.* Also, complete; utter, as a consummate bore.

compendium (kum pen' dē um) [COM together + PEND to weigh]—*lit.* that which is weighed together; a shortening or summary of a larger work. *The executive secretary wrote a brief compendium of the company's policies.*

ALSO: colloquial, colloquium, complacent, compulsive, concoction, concord, concourse, concur, concurrent, conducive, congregation, conjugal, conscription, conversant, corrupt

---

EXERCISE 1   Write the appropriate COM word.

1. His rate of promotion has not been _____ with his hard work.

2. The management won't _____ such sloppy work.

3. Her grades did not _____ with her IQ score.

4. He's a _____ salesman, the best in the company.

5. I felt no _____ about missing that meeting.

6. When their twins were born, they moved to a more _____ apartment.

7. No one was there to _____ with her when she needed sympathy most.

8. They traced the loss to _____ between two aides.

9. Here's a _____ of our report for those who don't want to read 300 pages.

10. The two engineers will _____ on the project.

11. The child's inability to speak was traced to a _____ defect.

12. They paid more for their _____ than they would have for a house.

13. Completely upset, she couldn't give a _____ account of the accident.

14. The committee will stop for lunch and _____ again at two.

15. Everyone at the party was in a _____ mood.

EXERCISE 2   REVIEW   Write C in front of each sentence in which all words are used correctly.

_____ 1. Anthropomorphism is still part of the culture of some African villages.

_____ 2. Winning the most important race was an anticlimax for her.

_____ 3. It was pleasant to watch the play in the outdoor amphitheater.

_____ 4. Because she was ambidextrous, she had to go in a wheelchair.

_____ 5. They celebrated their centennial wedding anniversary last month.

_____ 6. Our chairs are so antiquated that we want to buy new ones.

_____ 7. The father was an autocrat, with all the rest of the family bowing to his wishes.

EXERCISE 3   REVIEW   In this paragraph are nine words you've studied. Copy the words below and fill in the blanks. For one word, you know two roots; for the rest, you've learned only one. After you finish, reread the paragraph. Does your knowledge of roots give you a better understanding of the material?

Last weekend our biology class went to the lake to study bivalves, amphibians, and various other forms of marine life. On our way there we took a circuitous route through a wooded area and were dismayed to find the roadsides cluttered with bottles, plastic cartons, and other trash that isn't biodegradable. People seem ambivalent about our natural scenery. They like a beautiful countryside, yet they clutter it. They wouldn't condone messiness in their own yards, and yet they feel no compunction about tossing a bottle or a candy wrapper into the woods. It's a perennial problem, and it will be solved only when each individual develops a responsible attitude toward our natural scenery.

WORD	ROOT	ROOT MEANING	WORD MEANING
1. _____	_____	_____	_____
2. _____	_____	_____	_____
3. _____	_____	_____	
	_____	_____	_____
4. _____	_____	_____	_____
5. _____	_____	_____	_____
6. _____	_____	_____	_____
7. _____	_____	_____	_____
8. _____	_____	_____	_____
9. _____	_____	_____	_____

CRED—to believe

In the Middle Ages it was customary for the servants to carry the prepared food from the kitchen to a small side table in the dining hall, where, in front of the master and his guests, one of the servants would taste the food to show that it was not spoiled or poisoned. This side table came to be called a credence (belief or trust), and still today in France a side table is called a *crédence* and in Italy a *credenza*. Our English word **credence** no longer refers to our trust in the food we eat, but we still speak of having credence (belief or trust) in what we read and in what people tell us.

Note how the following CRED words go in pairs:

credible—believable
incredible—unbelievable

credulous—believing too readily
incredulous—not believing readily

credulity—tendency to believe readily
incredulity—tendency not to believe readily

credit—trust, as financial credit; a source of honor, as a credit to one's family
discredit [DIS not + CRED to believe]—*lit.* not to believe; to distrust; to destroy belief in
credentials—documents that cause others to believe in one
creed (also **credo**)—a formal statement of religious or other beliefs, as the creed of a church

credible (kred′ uh bul)—believable. *He gave a credible explanation for his tardiness.*
incredible (in kred′ uh bul) [IN not + CRED to believe]—unbelievable. *The amount of work she could do in an hour was incredible.*
credibility (kred uh bil′ uh tē)—reliability. *No one ever questioned his credibility.*
credulous (krej′ uh lus)—believing too readily on too little evidence; gullible. *Only a credulous person would be taken in by such ads.*
incredulous (in krej′ uh lus) [IN not + CRED to believe]—not believing readily; disbelieving. *When she heard she had won the prize, she was incredulous.*

credulity (kri doo′ li tē)—tendency to believe readily on too little evidence; gullibility. *Her credulity made her an easy prey for anyone with a hard luck story.*

incredulity (in kri doo′ li tē) [IN not + CRED to believe]—tendency not to believe readily; skepticism. *As he listened to the excuses, his incredulity was obvious.*

credence (krē′ duns)—belief; acceptance as true. *They gave little credence to the rumor.*

miscreant (mis′ krē unt) [MIS bad + CRED to believe]—originally, an unbeliever in religion; now, an evildoer or criminal. *The police were trying to round up the miscreants.*

ALSO: accreditation, accredited, creditor

EXERCISE 1 Write the appropriate CRED word.

1. The excuse he gave was simply not _____.
2. As some of the jurors began frowning, the lawyer became aware of their

   _____.

3. I wouldn't give any _____ to such a poorly documented report.

4. The _____ has so far evaded the police.
5. When they heard that their son had left the city, they were _____.

6. All his big stories taxed my _____.

7. I'm not so _____ as to believe all I'm told.

8. On his trek through the Arctic, he endured _____ hardships.
9. The jury questioned the _____ of the witness.

EXERCISE 2 Each day be sure to write a few sentences in your vocabulary journal using some of the new words you have learned.

CUR—to run (For CUR to care, see p. 151)

If you find it difficult to hang onto your money, don't be surprised because the word **currency** means literally *running*. The currency in circulation in a country is constantly *running* from person to person. And if currency should *run* through the hands of a person or a company too rapidly, it might be the **precursor** [PRE before + CUR to run] or forerunner of bankruptcy.

excursion [EX out + CUR to run]—*lit.* a running out somewhere; a short journey

current—the flow (running) of water or air or electricity; prevalent at the moment (running along), as current fashions

currency—money that passes (runs) from person to person in a country

curriculum—originally, a race course; today, all the courses offered by an educational institution

cursive—*lit.* running along; handwriting with the letters joined together

occur [OB toward + CUR to run]—*lit.* to run toward; to take place; to happen

courier—a messenger who carries (runs with) messages

corridor—a narrow hallway that runs through a building, often with rooms opening onto it

course—a running onward from one point to the next, as the course of a stream; in education, a series of studies leading (running) toward a degree

recur (ri kur´) [RE again + CUR to run]—*lit.* to run again; to happen again. *If the problem should recur, you'll have to buy a new battery.*

recurrent (ri kur´ unt) [RE back + CUR to run]—*lit.* running back; returning repeatedly. *They still had the recurrent problem of absenteeism.*

recourse (rē´ kōrs) [RE back + CUR to run]—*lit.* a running back (for help); a turning to someone for aid. *His only recourse was to notify the police.*

concur (kun kur´) [CON together + CUR to run]—*lit.* to run together; to agree. *We all concurred with the recommendation of the committee.*

concurrent (kun kur´ unt) [CON together + CUR to run]—*lit.* running together; occurring at the same time. *The town council and the school board held concurrent meetings.*

concourse (kon´ kōrs) [CON together + CUR to run]—*lit.* a running together; a great crowd; a large open space for the gathering of crowds. *The main concourse in the airport was filled with tourists.*

discourse (dis´ kōrs) [DIS apart + CUR to run]—*lit.* to run about; a formal and lengthy discussion of a subject. *He gave a discourse on Ibsen's symbolism.*

discursive (dis kur′ siv) [DIS apart + CUR to run]—*lit.* running apart; passing from one topic to another; rambling. *It was difficult to follow such a discursive lecture.*

cursory (kur′ suh rē)—running over rapidly without attention to detail; hasty and superficial. *She gave the novel only a cursory reading.*

precursor (pri kur′ sur) [PRE before + CUR to run]—a person or thing that runs before; a forerunner. *The fountain pen was the precursor of the ballpoint.*

ALSO: concurrence, incur, incursion, occurrence

EXERCISE 1   Write the appropriate CUR word.

1. Even a _____ glance at the program told her the music would not be rock.
2. Because the two meetings were _____, she couldn't attend both.
3. His _____ attacks of asthma led him to go to a specialist.
4. I _____ with all your suggestions and will help you carry them out.
5. Her writing was _____, never coming to the point.
6. Since nothing had been written about the invention, my only _____ was to seek an interview with the inventor.
7. On the prairies, the blossoming crocuses are a welcome _____ of spring.
8. Hundreds of strikers filled the _____ in front of the city hall.
9. He bored us with another of his _____ on the value of free trade.
10. He hoped that listening to ghost stories around the campfire wouldn't make his nightmares _____.

DEM—people

Many words have changed their meanings over the centuries, some having changed so much that they now mean almost the opposite of what they meant originally. **Demagogue** is an example. First used at the time of the Peloponnesian War, the word demagogue (DEM people + AGOG leader) referred to a leader or orator who championed the cause of the common *people* of Athens in their fight against the aristocrats of Sparta. Gradually through the years, however, such leaders began pursuing their own interests rather than helping the people. And today a demagogue is a political leader who makes impassioned appeals to the emotions and prejudices of *people* in order to gain power.

democracy [DEM people + CRAC to rule]—government by representatives elected by the people

epidemic [EPI upon + DEM people]—*lit.* upon the people; a disease or other abnormal condition spreading rapidly among many people

endemic (en dem' ik) [EN in + DEM people]—native to a particular people or country, as an endemic disease, which occurs only among certain people, or an endemic plant or animal, which is found only in a certain location. *The snail darter, an endangered species, is endemic to the Little Tennessee River.*

pandemic (pan dem' ik) [PAN all + DEM people]—*lit.* among all the people; widespread. *The depression was pandemic.*

demagogue (dem' uh gog) [DEM people + AGOG leader]—originally, a leader of the common people; now, a leader who stirs up the people by appealing to their emotions and prejudices in order to win them over quickly and thus gain power. *Interested only in gaining personal power, the senator was a demagogue.*

demagoguery (dem' uh gog uh rē) [DEM people + AGOG leader]—the methods or practices of a demagogue. *Her campaign speech was pure demagoguery.*

demographic (dem uh graf' ik) [DEM people + GRAPH to write]—*lit.* writing about people; pertaining to the study of human populations, especially their density, distribution, and vital statistics. *The 1980 census gathered a wealth of demographic information.*

ALSO: democrat, democratic, demography

44

EXERCISE 1 Write the appropriate DEM word.

1. Although the eucalyptus tree is _____ to Australia, years ago it was brought to California, where it now grows in many areas.

2. The politician was really a _____, seeking to advance his own interests.

3. People no longer have to fear a polio _____.

4. Concern about the threat of nuclear war has become _____.

5. _____ information is helpful in locating new enterprises.

6. Because he had no real issues to propose, the politician resorted to

   _____ to try to win votes.

EXERCISE 2 REVIEW Give the meaning of each root and a word in which it is found.

	MEANING	WORD
1. A, AN	_____	_____
2. AMBI, AMPHI	_____	_____
3. ANN, ENN	_____	_____
4. ANTE, ANTI	_____	_____
5. ANTHROP	_____	_____
6. ANTI	_____	_____
7. AUTO	_____	_____
8. BENE	_____	_____
9. BI	_____	_____
10. BIO	_____	_____
11. CHRON	_____	_____
12. CIRCUM	_____	_____
13. COM, CON, COL, COR	_____	_____
14. CRED	_____	_____
15. CUR	_____	_____
16. DEM	_____	_____

DICT—to speak

The word addict has had a long history. In Roman law, to addict a person meant to turn that person over to a master by sentence (*speaking*) of the court. Through the years addict has kept something of its old meaning in that it now refers to turning oneself over to a habit, which can, of course, be a master.

dictionary—a book containing the words of a (spoken) language

predict [PRE before + DICT to speak]—*lit.* to speak beforehand; to foretell

contradict [CONTRA against + DICT to speak]—to speak against; to assert the opposite of what someone has said

dictate—to speak or read something aloud to be recorded by another; to give (speak) orders or commands

dictator—one whose speech is to be taken as the final word; one who orders others around; a tyrannical ruler

dictatorial—speaking and acting in a domineering or oppressive way

valedictorian (val uh dik tōr′ ē un) [VALE farewell + DICT to speak]—a student, usually of the highest scholastic standing, who gives the farewell speech at commencement. *As valedictorian of her class, she gave a good speech at graduation.*

diction (dik′ shun)—choice of words in speaking or writing. *She used excellent diction, always choosing exactly the right word.* Also, enunciation in speaking or singing. *His diction was so clear that he could be understood at the back of the auditorium.*

jurisdiction (joor us dik′ shun) [JURIS law + DICT to speak]—the right to interpret (speak) and apply the law; legal power to hear and decide cases; the extent of such judicial or other authority. *The case was not within the court's jurisdiction.*

abdicate (ab′ di kāt) [AB away + DICT to speak, proclaim]—*lit.* to proclaim away; to renounce formally a throne or high office. *The king abdicated.*

addict (uh dikt′) [AD to + DICT to speak]—*lit.* to speak to or to sentence oneself; to give oneself habitually or compulsively to something. *He was addicted to alcohol.*

dictum (dik′ tum)—a formal and authoritative statement (speech). *After hearing the dictum of the chairperson, the committee members knew what they had to do.*

edict (ē′ dikt) [E out + DICT to speak]—*lit.* a speaking out; an official decree. *The Edict of Nantes granted toleration to Protestants in France.*

ALSO: addiction, benediction, ditto, interdict, malediction, verdict

EXERCISE 1 Write the appropriate DICT word.

1. The judge was overwhelmed by the number of cases in his _____.

2. She was trying to improve her _____ by taking a course in public speaking.

3. The head of the committee was _____, always trying to force decisions.

4. When the king _____, his son took the throne.

5. The residents of the island were granted citizenship by an _____ of the colonial government.

6. After the president's _____ about absenteeism, the employees complied with the new stricter rules.

7. His hard work paid off, and he became the _____ of his class.

8. She was _____ to soap operas, spending most of her time watching them.

EXERCISE 2 Are you keeping a WORD LIST on a blank page at the end of the book? Don't put down too many words. Just write those you are hoping to keep permanently in your vocabulary.

DIS, DI, DIF—not, away, apart

It was important in Roman times to start a journey or begin a new venture on a lucky day. One way to find out whether a day was favorable was to consult the stars. If the stars were *not* in a favorable position, the outcome of any undertaking begun on that day was certain to be a **disaster** (DIS not + ASTER star).

disaster [DIS not + ASTER star]—*lit.* the stars not in a favorable position; a misfortune

disease [DIS not + AISE ease]—*lit.* not at ease; illness

distract [DIS apart + TRACT to draw]—to draw away the attention

display [DIS apart + PLIC to fold]—*lit.* to fold apart or unfold; to show

divorce [DI away + VERS to turn]—*lit.* a turning away (in different directions); a dissolution of a marriage

diversion [DI away + VERS to turn]—something that turns the mind away and relaxes or entertains

diverse (di vurs′) [DI away + VERS to turn]—*lit.* turned away from each other; unlike, as diverse opinions

dissect [DIS apart + SECT to cut]—to cut apart, especially for anatomical study

dismantle [DIS apart + MANTEL cloak]—originally, to take a man's cloak off his back; to strip a house of furnishings; to take apart

disproportionate (dis pruh pawr′ shun it)—not proportionate; out of proportion in size, shape, or amount. *His salary was disproportionate to the amount of work he did.*

dissuade (di swād′) [DIS away + SUAD to persuade]—to turn a person away (from a course) by persuasion. *Finally they dissuaded him from giving up his job.*

disseminate (di sem′ uh nāt) [DIS apart + SEMIN seed]—to spread abroad as if sowing seed. *The publication disseminated information about endangered species.*

dissonant (dis′ uh nunt) [DIS apart + SON to sound]—*lit.* to sound apart; harsh or inharmonious; discordant. *One dissonant voice can ruin a choir.* Also, disagreeing. *Several dissonant opinions were expressed in the meeting.*

dissent (di sent′) [DIS apart + SENT to feel]—to differ in opinion or feeling; to withhold approval. *If too many members dissent, the motion will not pass.*

dissident (dis′ uh dunt) [DIS apart + SID to sit]—*lit.* sitting apart; disagreeing with an opinion or a group. *The dissident faction refused to* *participate in the project.* Also, one who disagrees; a dissenter. *The dissidents made trouble for the ruling party.*

disarray (dis uh rā') [DIS not + AREER to array]—*lit.* not arrayed or arranged properly; a state of disorder or confusion; disorderly dress. *Following the death of their leader, the political group fell into disarray.*

disconsolate (dis kon' suh lit)—not able to be consoled; hopelessly sad. *The team member responsible for losing the relay was disconsolate.*

disparity (di spar' uh tē) [DIS not + PAR equal]—difference; unlikeness. *In spite of the disparity in their ages, they get along well.*

disparate (dis' pur ut) [DIS not + PAR equal]—*lit.* not equal; unlike. *The reporter wrote on subjects as disparate as ice hockey and women's fashions.*

disconcert (dis kun surt') [DIS not + CONCERT to bring into agreement] —to upset; to frustrate. *The speaker was disconcerted by the noise in the balcony.*

discomfit (dis kum' fit) [DIS not + COM together + FAC to do]—*lit.* to undo; to thwart the plans of; to make uneasy. *The leader felt discomfited because his motives were being questioned.*

(Disconcert and discomfit are close synonyms.)

disburse (dis burs') [DIS away + BURSA a purse]—*lit.* to take away from a purse; to pay out, as from a fund. *The president of the society disbursed the scholarship funds.*

ALSO: diffident, diffuse, discord, discourse, discredit, discursive, dismiss, disparage, dispel, dispense, disrupt, dissolution, distort, diversity, divert

---

EXERCISE 1 Write the appropriate word beginning with DIS.

1. No one could _____ him from his goal.

2. Because she had not expected visitors, her house was in _____.

3. The members couldn't agree on who should _____ the funds.

4. The cult was trying to _____ its views through door-to-door canvassing.

5. The movie director was _____ or _____ by the bad reviews.

6. He _____ the room in preparation for a thorough cleaning.

7. There was considerable _____ between the brochure description of the condominium and its actuality.

8. The two students were writing on widely _____ subjects.

9. One _____ note marred an otherwise beautiful solo.

EQU—equal

If you want your fair or *equal* share of an estate, you want your **equity.** If you want a fair settlement of a legal case, you want an **equitable** settlement. If you're eager for spring, you're waiting for the spring **equinox,** when days and nights are *equal.* If you're looking for a climate that's *equally* pleasant in summer and winter, you're looking for an **equable** climate. And if you can remain *equally* calm and composed under pleasant or unpleasant circumstances, you're able to maintain your **equanimity.**

equalize—to make equal

equivalent—equal in value, force, or meaning

equator—a line equally distant at all points from the North and South Poles

equation—a statement in mathematics in which two quantities are equal

adequate [AD to + EQU equal]—equal to what is required; sufficient

equilibrium (ē kwuh lib′ rē um) [EQU equal + LIBR balance]—a state of balance between opposing forces. *When the horse swerved, the boy lost his equilibrium and fell off.*

equinox (ē′ kwuh noks) [EQU equal + NOX night]—*lit.* equal night; the time of year when the sun crosses the equator and day and night are of equal length. *The spring equinox on March 21 marks the beginning of spring.*

equilateral (ē kwuh lat′ ur ul) [EQU equal + LATER side]—having equal sides. *He drew an equilateral triangle on the board.*

equate (i kwāt′)—to represent as equal. *It's not possible to equate money and happiness.*

equity (ek′ wuh tē)—an ownership right to property. *Because they had paid so little on the mortgage, they had little equity in the house.* Also, something that is just, impartial, and fair. *He received his equity from his uncle's estate.*

equitable (ek′ wuh tuh bul)—reasonable; fair; just. *They achieved an equitable settlement out of court.*

equable (ek′ wuh bul)—equal at all times; unvarying. *Hawaii has an equable climate, equally pleasant in summer and winter.*

equanimity (ē kwuh nim′ uh tē) [EQU equal + ANIM mind]—evenness of mind or temper; composure. *No matter what happened, she always maintained her equanimity.*

equivocal (i kwiv′ uh kul) [EQU equal + VOC voice]—*lit.* having equal voices; capable of two interpretations. *Her equivocal reply was so carefully worded that the members of each faction thought she favored them.*

equivocate (i kwiv′ uh kāt) [EQU equal + VOC voice]—*lit.* to use equal voices; to make statements with two possible meanings in order to mislead. *The candidate equivocated so much that it was impossible to tell where he stood on any issue.*

ALSO: inadequate, inequality, inequity, iniquity, unequivocal

---

EXERCISE 1   Write the appropriate EQU word.

1. It's not always possible to _____ salary and job satisfaction.
2. Because he has so often _____, people are reluctant to believe him.
3. Having paid off the mortgage, we now have full _____ in our house.
4. His _____ in times of crisis was amazing.
5. While trying to get on my bike with my packages, I lost my _____.
6. Florida has a more _____ climate than Maine.
7. After the fall _____, the days get shorter.
8. The shape of the island was roughly that of an _____ triangle.
9. In giving an _____ answer, he tried to please everyone but actually pleased no one.
10. An _____ agreement was finally reached by the contractor and the builder.

EXERCISE 2   REVIEW   Write C in front of each sentence in which all words are used correctly.

_____   1. Radio and television make it easy to disseminate information quickly.
_____   2. Her excuse was so credible that no one believed her.
_____   3. It's usually possible to correlate vocabulary and success in college.
_____   4. A philanthropic person gives money to charitable causes.
_____   5. A commodious apartment would be a very modern one.
_____   6. A miscreant is an error in a manuscript.
_____   7. A bilateral agreement is written in two languages.
_____   8. A coherent speech is orderly and easy to follow.
_____   9. Perennial is the name of a flower.
_____ 10. He showed his incredulity by his raised eyebrows.
_____ 11. To circumvent is to open all the windows.

_____ 12. A condominium differs from an apartment mainly in that one owns it.

_____ 13. Her explanation, full of circumlocutions, never did come to the point.

_____ 14. We heard a long discourse on the dangers of food additives.

_____ 15. It was a convivial group that gathered for the holiday celebration.

_____ 16. To collaborate is to work together.

_____ 17. The supervisor went around to circumspect each employee's work.

_____ 18. A companion was originally a person one shared bread with.

_____ 19. A precursor is in charge of money matters on a ship.

_____ 20. A credulous person tends to believe without sufficient evidence.

_____ 21. No one could dissuade him from resigning.

_____ 22. A consensus is the recording of the population in an area.

_____ 23. To commiserate with someone is to sympathize.

_____ 24. His wild tales strain my credulity.

_____ 25. She's a consummate decorator, designing the finest interiors in the city.

_____ 26. The committee decided to convene until after lunch.

_____ 27. Her recurrent absences are giving her a bad reputation.

_____ 28. The dictum of the president left no room for argument.

_____ 29. She was delighted to have a supervisor who was not dictatorial.

_____ 30. Our country believes in the equity of all races.

_____ 31. To abdicate is to give up a throne or high office.

_____ 32. His attack of symbiosis was mild, and he soon recovered.

_____ 33. A cursory glance is a critical glance.

EXERCISE 3   REVIEW   These paragraphs contain ten words you've studied. Can you find all ten? Copy them below and fill in the blanks. For one word, you know two roots; for the rest, you've learned only one. When you finish, reread the paragraph and note how enjoyable the reading is when you know every word.

When I first came into this class, I was incredulous at the amount of work assigned. I almost lost my equanimity when I heard that we had to write a daily journal, and I wondered whether I could somehow circumvent the requirement. Soon, though, I realized that my attitude was atypical. The consensus of the class seemed to be that the professor is our benefactor.

For a while I was ambivalent, but finally my attitude changed until now it is the antithesis of what it was at first. I now concur with the opinion of the other students and find that I'm adding an incredible number of words to my vocabulary.

WORD	ROOT	ROOT MEANING	WORD MEANING
1. _____	_____	_____	_____
2. _____	_____	_____	_____
3. _____	_____	_____	_____
4. _____	_____	_____	_____
5. _____	_____	_____	_____
6. _____	_____	_____	_____
7. _____	_____	_____	_____
8. _____	_____	_____	_____
9. _____	_____	_____	_____
	_____	_____	_____
10. _____	_____	_____	_____

EU—good, well

If you are in a state of **euphoria,** you feel that life is *good,* that everything is going *well.* EU always means *good* or *well.* A **eulogy** is a speech that says *good* things about someone; **euphonious** prose has a pleasant (*good*) sound; and the controversial subject of **euthanasia** is concerned literally with a *good* death, a death for merciful reasons.

Do you ever use **euphemisms?** Look in the following list of EU words and find out.

eulogy (yoo′ luh jē) [EU good + LOG speech]—*lit.* a good speech; spoken or written praise of someone or something, especially praise of a person who has recently died. *He gave a moving eulogy at the funeral of his friend.*

eulogize (yoo′ luh jīz) [EU good + LOG speech]—*lit.* to give a good speech; to give a speech in praise of. *The man who had started the project was eulogized by all the speakers.*

euthanasia (yoo thuh nā′ zhuh) [EU good + THAN death]—*lit.* a good death; painless putting to death for merciful reasons, as in a terminal illness. *They were advocating a law permitting euthanasia for those who are suffering and cannot get well.*

euphemism (yoo′ fuh miz um)—the substitution of a mild (good) word in place of a distasteful or unpleasant one. *She spoke in euphemisms, talking of passing on rather than dying, of the departed rather than the dead, and of depressed areas rather than slums.*

euphony (yoo′ fuh nē) [EU good + PHON sound]—*lit.* good sound; a harmonious succession of words having a pleasing sound. *I like the euphony of the speeches of Martin Luther King, Jr.*

euphonious (yoo fō′ nē us) [EU good + PHON sound]—having a pleasant (good) sound; harmonious. *I listened to the euphonious sounds of the forest.*

euphoria (yoo fōr′ ē uh)—a feeling of well-being. *After she became engaged, she was in a state of euphoria.*

ALSO: eucalyptus, Eugene, eugenics

EXERCISE 1   List some more euphemisms.

EXERCISE 2   Write the appropriate EU word.

1. The speaker _____ the soldiers who had died but said little about those who were still living.
2. The sounds coming from the piano practice rooms were not exactly

   _____.

3. Antony's _____ after the death of Julius Caesar is one of the best-known passages in Shakespeare.
4. Instead of speaking of the poor, she always uses the _____ *underprivileged.*
5. I was in a state of _____ when I learned that I had been hired.

6. The _____ of the poetry of Robert Frost makes it pleasant to read aloud.
7. Capital punishment and _____ are widely debated issues.

EXERCISE 3   REVIEW   Write C in front of each sentence in which all words are used correctly.

_____ 1. I read a brief compendium of his extensive research paper.

_____ 2. A concourse is a Mickey Mouse course.

_____ 3. The doctor prescribed an anecdote for the snakebite.

_____ 4. The results weren't commensurate with the amount of work I put into the project.

_____ 5. On Tuesday morning the two senate committees held concurrent meetings.

_____ 6. The treasurer failed to disburse the funds in the scholarship account.

_____ 7. His talk was so discursive that it was easy to follow.

_____ 8. Her office is usually in disarray.

_____ 9. I was incredulous when I heard that she had quit her job.

_____ 10. They didn't condone their child's bad behavior.

_____ 11. Both cars were demolished in the collusion.

_____ 12. Magellan was the first to circumnavigate the globe.

_____ 13. Not a single dissonant opinion was expressed during the entire meeting.

_____ 14. The president would not tolerate any dissent.

EX, ES, E—out

Our word **escape** means breaking loose from any confinement, but originally it had a more picturesque meaning. In Roman times, perhaps when a jailor was trying to hang onto a prisoner by his cape, the prisoner slipped *out* of his cape and left it in the hands of the jailor. The prisoner had got "out of his cape"; he had escaped (ES out + CAP cape) and gone free.

escape [ES out + CAP cape]—*lit.* out of one's cape; to break out of confinement

export [EX out + PORT to carry]—to carry out of a country

expel [EX out + PEL to drive]—to drive out

exclaim [EX out + CLAM to shout]—*lit.* to shout out; to speak out suddenly

eject [E out + JECT to throw]—to throw out forcefully, as a landlord ejects a tenant

emit [E out + MIT to send]—to send out, as a child emits a yell or a factory emits smoke

excavate [EX out + CAV hollow]—to hollow out

educate [E out + DUC to lead]—*lit.* to lead out (draw out) the inborn abilities of a pupil; to develop or train

emigrate [E out + MIGRA to move]—to move out of a country (in contrast to immigrate, which means to move into a country)

erase [E out + RAS to scrape]—*lit.* to scrape out; to remove recorded material

exodus (ek' suh dus) [EX out + OD way]—*lit.* a way out; a departure, usually of a large number of people. *The exodus from the cities to the suburbs has caused much concern.*

exterminate (ek stur' muh nāt) [EX out + TERMINUS boundary]—*lit.* to put things out of the boundary; to destroy living things by killing off all individuals. *I'm trying to exterminate these cockroaches.*

eradicate (i rad' i kāt) [E out + RADIC root]—*lit.* to tear out by the roots; to destroy. *It's difficult to eradicate racial prejudice.*

extirpate (ek' stur pāt) [EX out + STIRPS root]—*lit.* to pull out by the roots; to destroy something completely by getting at the roots or causes so that it can't come to life again. *The commission hopes to extirpate the corruption in the police department.*

(The preceding three words are nearly synonymous. Exterminate means to destroy utterly and is usually applied to insects or people. Extirpate implies a violent rooting out and is often applied to a vice or crime. Eradicate implies a less violent uprooting and is applied to a disease or a fault or a prejudice.)

expurgate (eks' pur gāt) [EX out + PURG to clean]—*lit.* to clean out; to take out obscene or objectionable material. *The cast voted to expurgate a shocking scene from the play.*

efface (i fās') [E out + FAC face]—*lit.* to remove the face of; to wipe out. *Nothing could efface the memory of that crash.*

enervate (en' ur vāt) [E out + NERV nerve]—*lit.* to take out the nerve; to deprive of nerve, force, vigor; to weaken. *She found the hot, humid climate enervating.*

exonerate (eg zon' uh rāt) [EX out + ONER burden]—*lit.* to take the burden out; to free from a charge or from guilt. *The jury exonerated him.*

expatiate (ek spā' shē āt) [EX out + SPATIUM space, course]—*lit.* to wander out of the course; to digress; to speak or write at length. *The salesperson expatiated on the value of the product until everyone was bored.*

excoriate (ek skōr' ē āt) [EX out + COR skin]—*lit.* to strip the skin off; to denounce harshly. *The candidate excoriated his opponent, lashing out at him in his public speeches.*

emolument (i mol' yuh munt) [E out + MOL to grind]—originally, a miller's fee for grinding (out) grain; now, a payment for services rendered. *Even though she received no emolument, she liked doing the job.*

ebullient (i bool' yunt) [E out + BULL to bubble or boil]—bubbling out; overflowing with enthusiasm. *Her ebullient manner made her an entertaining lecturer.*

ALSO: edict, effusive, egregious, eloquent, elucidate, emissary, erupt, eventuate, evoke, exacerbate, excise, exclude, exculpate, expedite, extort

---

EXERCISE 1 Write the appropriate word beginning with EX, ES, E.

1. She found cold showers _____ rather than invigorating.

2. His later years of affluence could not _____ the memory of his early years of privation.

3. The accused was sure the evidence would _____ him.

4. The editor _____ the offensive language from the novel.

5. The kindergarten teacher's lively, _____ personality made the children love her.

6. The volunteers expected no _____ for their services.

7. She _____ at great length about her ailments.

8. Because the speaker was angry, he _____ those who disagreed with him.

FID—faith

Did you ever wonder how Fido got his name? He's called Fido because he's *faithful* to his master. The root FID always has something to do with *faith*. **Fidelity** means *faith*fulness, and **infidelity** means un*faith*fulness. If you are **confident,** you have *faith* in yourself, but if you are **diffident** [DI not + FID faith], you don't have *faith* in yourself; you are shy.

Sometimes, as in **confide** and several other words below, CON is used merely as an intensive, giving more emphasis to the root that follows.

confide [CON (intensive) + FID faith]—to show faith by sharing secrets
confident [CON (intensive) + FID faith]—having faith in oneself; self-assured

confidant (kon′ fuh dant) [CON (intensive) + FID faith]—*lit.* a person one has faith in; a person one confides it. *Her dad had been her confidant for years.*
diffident (dif′ uh dunt) [DIF not + FID faith]—not having faith in oneself; shy. *The youngster was diffident about speaking on the radio.*
fidelity (fi del′ uh tē)—faithfulness. *His fidelity to the party platform was unquestionable.*
infidelity (in fuh del′ uh tē) [IN not + FID faith]—unfaithfulness, especially in marriage. *No one had ever accused him of infidelity.*
infidel (in′ fuh dul) [IN not + FID faith]—*lit.* not faithful; a person who does not believe in a particular religion. *The Muslims were in conflict with the infidels.*
bona fide (bō′ nuh fīd) [BON good + FID faith]—*lit.* in good faith; genuine. *They made a bona fide offer on the house. The museum has a bona fide Gauguin painting.*
perfidious (per fid′ ē us) [PER through + FID faith]—deceiving through a pretense of faith; treacherous. *Her perfidious actions branded her as someone not to be trusted.*
perfidy (pur′ fuh dē) [PER through + FID faith]—deception through a pretense of faith; treachery. *They were shocked at the perfidy of the man who had seemed so honest.*

ALSO: affidavit, confidence, confidential

EXERCISE 1   Write the appropriate FID word.

1. He owned a _____ Model T Ford.

2. Even a _____ person will enjoy choral reading because one loses one's shyness in the group.

3. His _____ attempts to undermine the work of his own committee were shocking.

4. Anyone not following the state religion was called an _____.

5. You can be sure of his _____; he would never be unfaithful.

6. She needed a _____ with whom she could discuss her problems.

7. Everyone was shocked at the _____ of such a trusted employee.

EXERCISE 2   REVIEW   Write C in front of each correct statement.

_____ 1. Maintaining one's equanimity is maintaining one's poise and composure.

_____ 2. The anterior part of an animal is the hind part.

_____ 3. He was trying to exonerate the weeds in his garden.

_____ 4. To expurgate is to remove offensive language from written material.

_____ 5. Instead of going straight home they took a circuitous route.

_____ 6. To emit something is to leave it out.

_____ 7. To excoriate is literally to strip the skin off a person or, in other words, to denounce harshly.

_____ 8. The term restroom is a euphemism.

_____ 9. Discomfited and disconcerted both mean to be upset about something.

_____ 10. Equinox refers to an Eskimo dwelling.

_____ 11. The secretary felt circumscribed by all the regulations she had to follow.

_____ 12. I've been reading about the antebellum Underground Railroad, which helped slaves escape to the North.

EXERCISE 3   In your journal write some sentences with FID words.

GEN—race, birth, kind

In ancient mythology, when a child was born, a guardian spirit or **genius** (so named because it appeared at *birth*) was appointed to guide the person throughout life. Today, although we no longer believe we are given a guiding genius at birth, still we may have within us from *birth* a genius for something such as math or painting. Thus the ancient guiding genius has now become an exceptional intellectual or creative ability.

GEN has several meanings. First of all, it means *birth*—not only the *birth* of people but also the *birth* of things (an engine **generates** or gives *birth* to electricity) and the *birth* of ideas (angry words **engender** or give *birth* to hate whereas kind words engender love). GEN also indicates good *birth* or breeding (**gentleman, gentry, genteel, gentility,** and **generous**). And GEN also means *race*. If you are interested in your family history, you are interested in **genealogy**, the study of the ancestry of a family or *race*. And finally, GEN means a category or *kind* (a **genre** is a particular *kind* of literary or artistic composition).

generation—all the people born at about the same time
genius—in ancient mythology, a guardian spirit appointed at birth to
   guide a person; now, an exceptional intellectual or creative ability
generate—*lit.* to give birth to; to produce, as an engine generates power
hydrogen [HYDR water + GEN birth]—a gas so called because it generates (gives birth to) water by its combustion

gentleman—a man of good birth
gentry—people of good birth
genteel—displaying the qualities of good breeding or aristocratic birth
gentility—superior social status; good manners
generous—willing to share as would a person of good birth
genial—having a friendly and kindly manner

genesis (jen' uh sis)—the birth or coming into being of anything; origin;
   creation. *His many childhood pets were the genesis of his interest in
   zoology.*
progeny (proj' uh nē) [PRO forth + GEN birth]—children or descendants.
   His progeny inherited his ambition.
progenitor (prō jen' uh tur) [PRO forth + GEN birth]—a direct ancestor.
   Their zeal for social reform could be traced to their progenitor.
engender (in jen' dur)—*lit.* to give birth to; to develop; to bring forth, as
   ideas or feelings. *His handling of the problem engendered respect from
   his fellow workers.*

ingenious (in jēn′ yus) [IN in + GEN birth]—*lit.* having inborn talent; clever at contriving. *It took an ingenious architect to design a house for such a small lot.*

ingenuous (in jen′ yo͞o us) [IN in + GEN birth]—*lit.* freeborn, honest; showing innocent or childlike simplicity or gullibility. *She was completely ingenuous, never questioning anything she was told.*

gene (jēn)—an element of the germ plasm that transmits characteristics of the parents, and hence of the race, to the child. *Information stored in the genes determines an individual's eventual height.*

genetics (juh net′ iks)—the science of heredity. *Fruit flies are often used in experiments in genetics because they reproduce so quickly.*

genealogy (jē nē al′ uh jē) [GEN race + -LOGY study of]—*lit.* the study of race; the study of family descent. *After seeing "Roots," many people became interested in genealogy.*

genocide (jen′ uh sīd) [GEN race + CID to kill]—the systematic, planned killing of a racial, political, or cultural group. *Genocide is unthinkable in any civilized society.*

generic (juh ner′ ik)—general kind; commonly available; not protected by a trademark, as generic drugs. *She usually economizes by buying generic cereals instead of name brands.*

genre (zhahn′ ruh)—a particular kind or category of literature or art. *He hadn't limited his reading to a single genre but had delved into poetry, the short story, and the novel.*

ALSO: congenital, cryptogenic, degenerate, eugenics, general, heterogeneous, homogeneous, homogenize, pathogenic, primogeniture, psychogenic

---

EXERCISE 1 Write the appropriate GEN word.

1. The Montgomery bus boycott was the _____ of the Civil Rights Movement.
2. I've been recording all the dates I can find for our family _____.
3. His kindness to the stranger will probably _____ friendship.
4. Their _____ came over from Germany a century ago.
5. She chose the short story as her particular _____ for study.
6. He had so many grandchildren and great-grandchildren that he had lost count of all his _____.
7. Her _____ answers showed her childlike innocence.
8. Only someone with delusions of racial superiority would contemplate _____.

GRAPH, GRAM—to write

We don't usually think of **geography** as having anything to do with writing, but it is made up of GEO, *earth*, and GRAPH, to *write*, and is actually a *writing* about the surface of the earth. Note how each of the following common words has something to do with *writing*.

diagram [DIA through + GRAM to write]—*lit.* a writing to show through something, to make it plain

telegram [TELE far + GRAM to write]—*lit.* far writing; a message sent by electric impulses through a wire or converted into radio waves

program [PRO before + GRAM to write]—a writing beforehand; a listing of things to follow; a printed announcement of events; in computer science, a sequential set of commands to be followed by a computer

geography [GEO earth + GRAPH to write]—a writing about the earth's surface

autograph [AUTO self + GRAPH to write]—*lit.* the writing of oneself; one's signature

stenographer [STEN narrow + GRAPH to write]—*lit.* one who uses narrow or small writing (shorthand)

monogram (mon' uh gram) [MONO one + GRAM to write]—two or more letters entwined (written) into one design. *On each towel she embroidered a monogram.*

monograph (mon' uh graf) [MONO one + GRAPH to write]—a book written about one specific subject. *She published a monograph about the Biblical references in Browning's poems.*

epigram (ep' uh gram) [EPI on + GRAM to write]—*lit.* a writing on a subject; any short, witty saying. *She liked to quote the epigram "Success is getting what you want; happiness is wanting what you get."*

cardiogram (kahr' dē uh gram) [CARD heart + GRAM to write]—a written tracing showing the contractions of the heart. *The cardiogram showed a deviation in the heart beat.*

graphic (graf' ik)—full of vivid details. *The author gave a graphic description of the earthquake.*

graphite (graf' īt)—a soft, black, lustrous form of carbon found in nature and used for lead in pencils (for writing). *Graphite has many other uses besides supplying the lead for pencils.*

graffiti (gra fē' tē)—crude drawings or writings scratched on public walls. *Getting rid of graffiti on the subway walls was the next civic project.*

choreography (kōr ē og' ruh fē) [CHOR dance + GRAPH to write]—*lit.* the writing of a story in dance; the creating and arranging of dance movements, especially ballet. *The director of the opera also did the choreography.*

topography (tuh pahg′ ruh fē) [TOP place + GRAPH to write]—a detailed drawing (writing) on a map of the surface features of a region (place). *Before venturing into the canyon, the hikers studied its topography.*

calligraphy (kuh lig′ ruh fē) [CALLI beautiful + GRAPH to write]—the art of fine handwriting. *She copied a favorite poem in beautiful calligraphy and had it framed.*

seismograph (sīz′ muh graf) [SEISMOS earthquake + GRAPH to write]—an instrument for recording (writing) the intensity and duration of an earthquake. *The seismograph recorded an earthquake of 7 on the Richter scale.*

ALSO: autobiography, bibliography, biography, cryptography, demographic, lithography, orthography, phonograph, photography, telegraph

---

EXERCISE 1   Write the appropriate GRAPH, GRAM word.

1. To make her writing true to life, she used many _____ details.

2. Her stationery was decorated with her _____.

3. The _____ of the Tchaikovsky ballet was entirely new.

4. A study of the _____ of the region showed many caves and hills.

5. The heart specialist explained to the patient the meaning of the jiggles on

   the _____.

6. The fence around the construction was covered with amusing _____.

7. The professor wrote a _____ about his research on cloning.

8. My aunt kept quoting the _____ "A place for everything, and everything in its place."

9. The course in _____ had taught her to write in artistic script.

10. I never knew before that the "lead" in pencils is actually _____.

11. The intensity of the earthquake was recorded by the _____.

LOG—speech, word

Words containing the root LOG have to do with *speech*. A **monologue** is a *speech* by one person. A **dialogue** is *speech* between two people. A **prologue** is a *speech* before a play, and an **epilogue** is a *speech* after it. (Note that most of these words can also be spelled without the *ue* ending.)

dialogue [DIA between + LOG speech]—speech between two people; a conversational passage in a play or narrative

travelogue—a speech or film about travel

apology [APO away + LOG speech]—*lit.* a speaking away; a speech expressing regret for a fault or offense

logic—the science of correct reasoning (speaking)

monologue (mon′ uh log) [MONO one + LOG speech]—a speech by one person; a soliloquy. *The monologue beginning "Is this a dagger which I see before me?" helps reveal Macbeth's character.*

prologue (prō′ log) [PRO before + LOG speech]—a speech before a play. Romeo and Juliet *begins with a prologue that summarizes the story for the audience.* Also, any introductory event. *The fancy appetizers were the prologue to an excellent dinner.*

epilogue (ep′ uh log) [EPI on + LOG speech]—a speech directed to the audience at the conclusion of a play. *Shakespeare's plays often end with an epilogue spoken by one of the characters.*

doxology (dok sol′ uh jē) [DOX praise + LOG speech]—a hymn or expression of praise to God. *The best-known doxology is the one sung in most Protestant churches, beginning "Praise God from whom all blessings flow."*

analogy (uh nal′ uh jē) [ANA according to + LOG speech, reason]—resemblance in some particulars between things otherwise unlike. *To get his point across, the professor used the following analogy: cutting classes is like paying for a hamburger and then walking away without eating it.*

analogous (uh nal′ uh gus) [ANA according to + LOG speech, reason]—similar in a way that permits the drawing of an analogy. *The wings of a bird and those of an airplane are analogous, having a similar function but a different origin and structure.*

ALSO: decalogue, eulogy, neologism

EXERCISE 1   Write the appropriate LOG word.

1. The _____ at the end of the play pointed out the moral.
2. It was hard to get a word in because his conversation was really a

   _____.
3. Her first complaint was just a _____ to what was to come.
4. The lecturer made each point clear by using an _____.
5. The witty _____ between the characters made *The Taming of the Shrew* famous.
6. Reading a book is _____ to dropping chemicals into a test tube; there should be a reaction.

EXERCISE 2   A dull subject can often be made more vivid and interesting by using an analogy. Note how effectively an analogy is used in this sentence from *Time: Like a pilot bailing out of a flaming aircraft and then waiting terror-stricken to see if his parachute will open, American businessmen and economists hung impatiently last week trying to see how deep the recession would go.*

In your vocabulary journal make up an analogy that you might use in some of your writing.

EXERCISE 3   REVIEW   Write C in front of each correct statement.

_____ 1. Infidelity means unfaithfulness, particularly in marriage.
_____ 2. A seismograph measures the size of an object.
_____ 3. Euphoria is a feeling of well-being.
_____ 4. A genre is a particular category of literature or art.
_____ 5. Euphony is something false.
_____ 6. An epigram is a short, witty saying.
_____ 7. Choreography is the arranging of dance movements.
_____ 8. The beagle Snoopy in "Peanuts" is an anthropomorphic character.
_____ 9. She's a good switch hitter because she's ambidextrous.

-LOGY—study of

-LOGY at the end of a word usually means *study of.* **Biology** [BIO life] is the *study of* plant and animal life. **Geology** [GEO earth] is the *study of* the history of the earth, especially as recorded in rocks. **Etymology** [ETYM true] is the *study of* the origin (true meaning) and development of words. In this book you are getting an introduction to etymology.

Almost all such words have O in front of the -LOGY so that the ending is -OLOGY. But two words have A in front of the -LOGY—genealogy and mineralogy.

geology (jē ol′ uh jē) [GEO earth + -LOGY study of]—the study of the history of the earth, especially as recorded in rocks. *The geology of the Grand Canyon shows the various periods in the earth's development.*

psychology (sī kol′ uh jē) [PSYCH mind + -LOGY study of]—the study of mental processes and behavior. *His study of psychology helped him understand himself.*

archeology (ahr kē ol′ uh jē) [ARCH ancient + -LOGY study of]—the study of ancient cultures based on artifacts and other remains. *Egypt is a good place to study archeology because the remains are well preserved.*

astrology (uh strol′ uh jē) [ASTR star + -LOGY study of]—a pseudoscience claiming to foretell the future by a study of the stars. *To try to foresee her future, she consulted a book on astrology.*

ecology (ē kol′ uh jē) [ECO home + -LOGY study of]—the study of the relationship between organisms and their environment (home). *The ecology of the region showed that the number of wild animals had decreased as a result of lumbering.*

ornithology (awr nuh thol′ uh jē) [ORNITH bird + -LOGY study of]—the scientific study of birds as a branch of zoology. *His interest in ornithology led him to make recordings of bird songs.*

meteorology (mē tē uh rol′ uh jē) [METEORA things in the air + -LOGY study of]—the study of the atmosphere, especially weather and weather conditions. *The Bureau of Meteorology is recording slight changes in climate from year to year.*

embryology (em brē ol′ uh jē)—the study of the formation and development of embryos. *The science of embryology has determined the exact times when various parts of the embryo develop.*

entomology (en tuh mol′ uh jē) [EN in + TOM to cut + -LOGY study of]—the study of insects (whose bodies are "cut" in three segments). *The entomology class was studying grasshoppers.*

etymology (et uh mol′ uh jē) [ETYM true + -LOGY study of]—the study of the origin (true meaning) and development of words. *From his study of etymology, he learned many interesting word histories.*

ALSO: anthropology, bacteriology, biology, chronology, dermatology, genealogy, gynecology, mineralogy, morphology, paleontology, pathology, physiology, technology, theology, zoology

---

EXERCISE 1 What science makes a study of the following?

1. the human mind _____

2. weather conditions _____

3. the origin and development of words _____

4. the history of the earth as recorded in rocks _____

5. ancient cultures based on remains _____

6. insects _____

7. birds _____

8. embryos _____
9. the relationship of organisms to their environment _____

EXERCISE 2 In this book you have been studying etymology. List three words —and the etymology of each—that you have found most interesting.

EXERCISE 3 Add a few more words to your WORD LIST on a blank page at the end of the book. Record words that you hope to use in conversation or in writing.

LOQU, LOC—to speak

A **soliloquy** [SOL alone + LOQU to speak] is a *speech* given by an actor, alone on the stage, to reveal private thoughts and emotions. The most famous soliloquy, of course, is Hamlet's "To be or not to be," when Hamlet reveals his feelings to the audience. Another soliloquy from a Shakespearean play is the opening *speech* of *Richard III*, "Now is the winter of our discontent. . . ."

soliloquy (suh lil' uh kwē) [SOL alone + LOQU to speak]—a speaking alone to oneself, as in a drama; a monologue. *The soliloquy is used less frequently in modern drama than in earlier plays.*

eloquent (el' uh kwunt) [E out + LOQU to speak]—*lit.* speaking out; fluent; persuasive. *The audience was moved by the eloquent speaker.*

colloquial (kuh lō' kwē ul) [COL together + LOQU to speak]—like the language used when people speak together informally; informal or conversational. *"Passing the buck" is a colloquial expression for "shifting responsibility."*

colloquium (kuh lō' kwē um) [COL together + LOQU to speak]—*lit.* a speaking together; an academic seminar on some field of study, led by several experts. *They attended the colloquium on Hemingway.*

loquacious (lō kwā' shus)—talkative. *It was my luck to get a loquacious partner at bridge.*

grandiloquent (gran dil' uh kwunt) [GRAND grand + LOQU to speak]—marked by a lofty, extravagantly colorful style. *The Duke tries to impress Huckleberry Finn with his grandiloquent speech.*

ventriloquist (ven tril' uh kwist) [VENTR stomach + LOQU to speak]—*lit.* one who speaks from the stomach; one who speaks so that the sounds seem to come from somewhere other than the speaker's mouth. *The ventriloquist was able to speak without moving his lips.*

ALSO: circumlocution, colloquy, elocution, eloquence, interlocutor, loquacity, obloquy

EXERCISE 1   Write the appropriate LOQU, LOC word.

1. She was so _____ that no one else had a chance to say anything.
2. He uses a _____ rather than a formal style of writing.
3. The politician hoped his _____ style of speaking, with big words and impressive gestures, would make up for his lack of ideas.
4. A dramatist may reveal a character's feelings to the audience through a

   _____.

5. The man with the puppet on his knee was a _____.
6. Six professors took part in the _____ on hazardous waste.

EXERCISE 2   List three colloquial expressions and their formal equivalents.

EXERCISE 3   REVIEW   Write C in front of each sentence in which all words are used correctly.

_____ 1. The gramophone was the precursor of the stereo.
_____ 2. A high school course in botany is often the genesis of a lifelong interest in plants.
_____ 3. The suit for divorce accused him of gentility.
_____ 4. To feel some compunction about something you have done is to feel a slight regret about it.
_____ 5. Meteorology has now made weather prediction more accurate.
_____ 6. Always interested in butterflies, she decided to major in entomology.
_____ 7. They were repainting the fence to get rid of the objectionable graffiti.
_____ 8. A disconsolate person tries to comfort others.
_____ 9. A confidant is a person one confides in.
_____ 10. Through the study of genetics, scientists are making discoveries about heredity.
_____ 11. A bona fide antique is a genuine antique.
_____ 12. Diffident means various kinds.

MAL—bad

In the medieval calendar, two days in each month were marked as *dies mali* (evil days)—January 1 and 25, February 4 and 26, March 1 and 28, April 10 and 20, May 3 and 25, June 10 and 16, July 13 and 22, August 1 and 30, September 3 and 21, October 3 and 22, November 5 and 28, and December 7 and 22. Any enterprise begun on one of these *bad days* was certain to end in failure. Our word **dismal** comes from *dies mali*, but today a dismal day is merely gloomy or depressing.

Was he really ill when he stayed at home from work during the week of the World Series, or was he just malingering? **Malinger** originally meant to be in *bad* health, but, as with many words, it has changed over the years and now means to pretend to be ill in order to avoid duty or work. Anyone who stays home from work pretending to be ill is malingering. If you claim you have a bad back when the walks need shoveling, if you develop a headache when you're supposed to go to a boring party, if you are too weary after dinner to help with the dishes—you could be malingering.

malnutrition—bad nutrition
maltreated—badly treated
maladjusted—badly adjusted to the circumstances of one's life
malpractice—improper treatment of a patient by a physician
malfunction—to function badly, as an engine malfunctions
malodorous—having a bad odor
dismal [DIES day + MAL bad]—depressing; dark and gloomy

malicious (muh lish′ us)—intentionally bad or harmful. *She refused to listen to malicious gossip.*

malice (mal′ is)—active bad feeling or ill will. *The incumbent felt no malice toward the person who defeated him.*

malcontent (mal′ kun tent)—*lit.* one who is badly contented; a discontented or rebellious person. *He was a born malcontent, always complaining.*

malady (mal′ uh dē)—*lit.* a bad condition; a disease. *Science has reduced the number of incurable maladies.*

malaria (muh ler′ ē uh) [MAL bad + AER air]—a disease once thought to be caused by bad air from the swamps. *Malaria is often contracted in the tropics.*

malignant (muh lig′ nunt)—bad or harmful; likely to cause death. *The biopsy revealed that the growth was not malignant.*

malign (muh līn′)—to speak evil of; to slander. *In the political debate his opponent maligned him.*

malevolent (muh lev′ uh lunt) [MAL bad + VOL to wish]—wishing evil toward others. *The defendant cast a malevolent glance toward his accuser.*

malinger (muh ling′ gur)—to pretend to be in bad health to get out of work. *Since his headaches always occurred just at schooltime, we knew he was malingering.*

malediction (mal uh dik′ shun) [MAL bad + DICT to speak]—a curse (opposite of benediction). *The leader of the cult pronounced a malediction upon all those who did not follow him.*

malfeasance (mal fē′ zuns) [MAL bad + FAC to do]—wrongdoing, especially by a public official. *The mayor was accused of malfeasance in his distribution of public funds.*

malefactor (mal uh fak′ tur) [MAL bad + FAC to do]—an evildoer; a criminal. *The police were looking for the malefactor.*

maladroit (mal uh droit′)—not adroit; not skillful; awkward; clumsy. *The new supervisor was maladroit in dealing with the employees.*

malaise (mal āz′) [MAL bad + AISE ease]—a vague feeling of illness or depression. *As she was preparing for the interview, a slight malaise came over her.*

malapropism (mal′ uh prop iz uhm)—*lit.* badly appropriate; not appropriate; a ludicrous misuse of a word that sounds somewhat like the word intended. (From Sheridan's play *The Rivals* in which Mrs. Malaprop misuses words humorously, as when she speaks of a shrewd awakening instead of a rude awakening.) *Archie Bunker made television viewers of the 70s laugh at his malapropisms, as when he said, "The donor may wish to remain unanimous."*

ALSO: malformed, malocclusion

EXERCISE 1   Write the appropriate MAL word.

1. Having used up his sick leave, he was no longer tempted to _____.

2. He suffered from one _____ after another.

3. The staff got tired of the complaints of the _____.

4. Her _____ gossip about her opponent was uncalled-for.

5. They had feared the tumor was _____, but it was benign.

6. She tried to _____ her fellow workers, saying untrue things about them.

7. Even so, they felt no _____ toward her.

8. The witch doctor pronounced a _____ upon his enemies.

9. The party boss was accused of _____ in using the party funds.

10. He avoided the _____ glances of his opponent.

11. As the time for his speech approached, his feeling of _____ increased.

12. Her bungling way of handling the problem was _____ to say the least.

13. In her attempt to use big words, she often used _____.

14. The _____ had so far evaded the detectives.

EXERCISE 2 In *The Rivals* Mrs. Malaprop says that Lydia is as headstrong as an allegory on the banks of the Nile. What word did she intend to use? List some malapropisms you have heard.

EXERCISE 3 REVIEW Write C in front of each sentence in which all words are used correctly.

_____ 1. I find jogging enervating and always feel full of energy afterward.

_____ 2. His perfidy was shocking because he had been such a trusted employee.

_____ 3. I give little credence to the testimony of such an untrustworthy witness.

_____ 4. In his study of his genealogy, he discovered that his ancestors had once lived in Holland.

_____ 5. Concern about what is happening to our environment has led to a new interest in the study of ecology.

_____ 6. The suit against him charged him with fidelity to the company he worked for.

EXERCISE 4 REVIEW Copy the underlined words on the lines below and fill
in the blanks. For one word, you know two roots; for the rest, you've learned
only one. When you finish, you should find it satisfying to reread the paragraph and get its full meaning.

Our political <u>conventions</u> are a <u>graphic</u> example of our <u>democracy</u> at
work. Before the convention, the platform <u>committee</u> must reach a <u>con-
sensus</u> on a platform that will be <u>ambiguous</u> enough to avoid offending
anyone, yet strong enough to <u>engender</u> support. At the convention itself,
<u>grandiloquent</u> speeches <u>eulogize</u> the candidates and <u>malign</u> the oppo-
sition. Finally, although the actual choice of a candidate is often an
<u>anticlimax</u> because the outcome has been known all along, the conven-
tion does answer the <u>perennial</u> human question, "Who shall lead?"

WORD	ROOT	ROOT MEANING	WORD MEANING
1.			
2.			
3.			
4.			
5.			
6.			
7.			
8.			
9.			
10.			
11.			
12.			

METER, METR—measure

Although for years Americans have used the root METER in such words as **thermometer, barometer, speedometer,** and **odometer,** they are dragging their feet in adopting the **metric system.** Only four other countries in the world don't use metric: Brunei, Burma, Yemen Arab Republic, and People's Democratic Republic of Yemen. But now, with many states requiring metric instruction in the schools, perhaps we will eventually go along with the rest of the metric world.

barometer [BAR pressure + METER measure]—an instrument for measuring atmospheric pressure

geometry [GEO earth + METR measure]—*lit.* earth measuring; originally, the system of measuring distances on earth through the use of angles; now, a branch of mathematics that deals with points, lines, planes, and solids

metric system—a decimal system of weights and measures based on the meter as a unit length and the kilogram as a unit mass

kilometer (kil′ uh mē tur) [KILO thousand + METER measure]—1000 meters; approximately 0.62 mile. *In Canada the speed limits are posted in kilometers.*

odometer (ō dom′ uh tur) [OD road + METER measure]—*lit.* a road measure; an instrument for measuring the distance traveled by a vehicle. *His policy was to trade in his car when the odometer registered 50,000 miles.*

pedometer (pi dom′ uh tur) [PED foot + METER measure]—an instrument that measures the distance walked by recording the number of steps taken. *To make sure she walked two miles a day, she took a pedometer with her.*

perimeter (puh rim′ uh tur) [PERI around + METER measure]—the boundary around an area. *An old rail fence ran along the perimeter of his farm.*

parameter (puh ram′ uh tur) [PARA beside + METER measure]—a fixed limit or boundary. *Stay within the parameters of the present budget.*
(Parameter, originally a mathematical term, is now used generally to indicate a fixed limit or boundary, but this usage is not yet considered standard by many authorities.)

tachometer (ta kom′ i tur) [TACH speed + METER measure]—an instrument used to measure speed, especially the revolutions per minute, of a revolving shaft. *My "tach" showed that my motor was revolving too fast.*

trigonometry (trig uh nom′ uh trē) [TRI three + GON angle + METR measure]—the branch of mathematics that deals with the relations between the sides and angles of triangles and the calculations based on these. *Her knowledge of trigonometry was of value in her surveying job.*

symmetrical (si met′ ri kul) [SYM together + METR measure]—*lit.* measured together; having both sides exactly alike. *He made a symmetrical flower arrangement for the center of the table.*

metronome (met′ ruh nōm) [METR measure + NOM law]—a clocklike instrument for measuring the exact time (law) in music by a regularly repeated tick. *Practicing the piano with a metronome helped her keep perfect time.*

ALSO: asymmetrical, centimeter, chronometer, diameter, isometric, micrometer, pentameter, telemetry, thermometer

---

EXERCISE 1 What word containing the root METER, METR names or de‧ scribes the following?

1. the boundary around an area _____

2. an instrument that measures atmospheric pressure _____

3. an instrument for measuring the distance traveled by a vehicle _____

4. approximately 0.62 mile _____
5. an instrument that measures time in music by a regularly repeated tick

_____

6. an instrument that measures the distance walked by recording the number

of steps taken _____

7. having both sides exactly alike _____

8. a fixed limit or boundary _____
9. an instrument used to measure the revolutions per minute of a revolving

shaft _____

EXERCISE 2 REVIEW Underline the appropriate word.

1. He spent a (disproportionate, diverse) amount of time on the first part of the book.

2. The students were bored as the professor (expatiated, equivocated) about his pet theory.

3. Instead of reading my report carefully, the supervisor gave it only a (dictatorial, cursory) glance.

4. After consulting many old records, she learned what country the family (progenitor, progeny) had come from.

MIT, MIS, MISS—to send

The MIT, MIS, MISS root has to do with sending. A **mission** is a task that one is *sent* to do. A **missionary** is someone *sent* out to do religious work. A **message** is a communication *sent* to someone. **Missive** is another word for a message that is *sent*, and the person with whom the message is *sent* is a **messenger**.

transmit [TRANS across + MIT to send]—to send (across) from one place or person to another

omit [OB away + MIT to send]—*lit.* to send away; to leave out

permit [PER through + MIT to send]—*lit.* to send through; to allow

dismiss [DIS away + MISS to send]—to send away

mission—a task that one is sent to do

missionary—one sent out to do religious work

missile—a weapon that is fired or otherwise sent toward a target

promise [PRO forth + MIS to send]—*lit.* to send forth; to indicate what may be expected

message—a communication sent to someone

messenger—a person with whom a message is sent

emissary (em′ uh ser ē) [E out + MISS to send]—a person sent out on a specific mission. *The government sent an emissary to look into the matter.*

missive (mis′ iv)—a letter or message that is sent. *A missive from the president directed their next move.*

transmission (trans mish′ un) [TRANS across + MISS to send]—a device that sends (across) power from the engine of an automobile to the wheels. *The transmission in his car is giving him trouble.* Also, the act of transmitting. *Their office requested immediate transmission of the document.*

intermittent (in tur mit′ unt) [INTER between + MIT to send]—*lit.* sent between intervals; stopping and starting at intervals. *The intermittent rain didn't prevent them from enjoying the game.*

premise (prem′ is) [PRE before + MIS to send]—*lit.* a statement sent before; an initial statement that is assumed to be true and upon which an argument is based. *His argument failed because he started with a false premise.*

demise (di mīz′) [DE away + MIS to send]—*lit.* sent away; death. *The demise of the leader ended the project.*

ALSO: admit, commission, commit, commitment, committee, emit, intermission, omission, remiss, remission, remit, submit

EXERCISE 1   REVIEW   Write C in front of each sentence in which all words are used correctly.

_____ 1. Graphic writing uses vivid details.

_____ 2. An infidel is a Cuban revolutionary.

_____ 3. Ornithology is the study of birds.

_____ 4. Colloquial expressions should not be used in formal writing.

_____ 5. A malefactor is a criminal.

_____ 6. The play _Our Town_ ends with a monologue between Emily and her mother.

_____ 7. A loquacious person talks too much.

_____ 8. A prologue comes at the beginning of a play and an epilogue at the end.

_____ 9. It was once thought that malaria was caused by bad air.

_____ 10. Archeology is the study of the remains of ancient civilizations.

_____ 11. Malaise is a vague feeling of illness or depression.

_____ 12. Malingering means lingering too long over meals.

_____ 13. To extirpate is to dig out by the roots.

_____ 14. Your pedometer tells you how far you have driven.

_____ 15. In Shakespearean plays one actor often speaks alone in a soliloquy.

_____ 16. She noted by her odometer that she was going over 55.

_____ 17. A malcontent is chronically unhappy.

_____ 18. Malicious gossip is amusing but never harmful.

_____ 19. An equivocal answer could be interpreted two ways.

_____ 20. A climate with little change the year around is called equable.

_____ 21. He was afraid to use big words for fear he'd use a malapropism.

_____ 22. Parameter means the distance around a property.

_____ 23. Engender refers to a male/female relationship.

_____ 24. The judge had a benign attitude toward first offenders.

_____ 25. In a state of eulogy, they planned their wedding.

_____ 26. Jurisdiction is the extent of judicial authority.

_____ 27. They have diverse interests; he likes music and she likes sports.

_____ 28. The final location of the factory will depend on demographic facts.

_____ 29. The lawyer claimed his client was amoral and didn't know that what he had done was wrong.

_____ 30. Our supervisor always gives us ambiguous instructions so that we know exactly what she wants us to do.

MONO—one

There are two roots meaning *one*—UNI (p. 176) and MONO. MONO is found in such words as **monoplane** (having only *one* pair of wings), **monarchy** (having *one* ruler), and **monotheism** (belief in *one* God). Two words we don't usually think of as containing MONO are monk and monastery. A **monk** was originally *one* religious man living alone, and a **monastery** was a dwelling place for monks, each *one* living alone.

monoplane—an airplane with only one pair of wings

monarchy [MONO one + ARCH ruler]—a government with one hereditary ruler

monopoly [MONO one + POLY to sell]—exclusive control by one group for selling a commodity or service

monk—originally, one religious man living alone; now, a member of a religious brotherhood living in a monastery

monastery—originally, a dwelling place for monks, each one living alone; now, the dwelling place of monks living in seclusion

monotonous [MONO one + TON tone]—*lit.* one tone; having no variation

monotone (mon′ uh tōn) [MONO one + TON tone]—having one tone; lack of variety in tone. *Because the professor always spoke in a monotone, his students fell asleep.*

monosyllable (mon′ uh sil uh bul)—a word of one syllable. *She thought she had to speak to the child in monosyllables.*

monocle (mon′ uh kul) [MONO one + OCUL eye]—an eyeglass for one eye. *The English gentleman looked at us through his monocle.*

monotheism (mon′ uh thē iz um) [MONO one + THE god]—the belief that there is only one God. *Unlike their neighbors, the early Hebrews held to monotheism.*

monogamy (muh nog′ uh mē) [MONO one + GAM marriage]—marriage to only one person at a time. *Monogamy is practiced in most countries today.*

monolith (mon′ uh lith) [MONO one + LITH stone]—one single large piece of stone, as a monument or a statue. *The monoliths at Stonehenge were transported from a great distance in prehistoric times.*

monolithic (mon uh lith′ ik) [MONO one + LITH stone]—like one single stone, hence solid, massive, and uniform. *The corporation had become monolithic with one strong central organization.*

ALSO: monochromatic, monogamist, monogram, monograph, monologue, mononucleosis, monoplane, monopolize, monorail, monotony

EXERCISE 1 Write the appropriate MONO word.

1. At least it's easy to tell where the accent falls in a _____.

2. _____ is the central belief of Christians, Jews, and Muslims.

3. Her speeches are boring because she speaks in a _____.

4. The primitive tribe practiced _____ and had strong taboos against marital infidelity.

5. The company was _____, with a reputation for uniform policy in all its branches.

6. In Tonga we saw huge _____ that had been set up in prehistoric times.

EXERCISE 2 REVIEW Write C in front of each sentence in which all words are used correctly.

_____ 1. Many people think there should be a law permitting euthanasia.

_____ 2. After I dismantled my typewriter, I couldn't put it back together again.

_____ 3. Her towels were embroidered with her monogram.

_____ 4. The new plastic heart in his body ticked like a metronome.

_____ 5. "All leaves are green" would be a false premise.

_____ 6. They studied a map showing the topography of the land they were entering.

_____ 7. A cardiogram is a short, witty saying.

_____ 8. The governor issued an edict forbidding government workers to strike.

_____ 9. Intermittent showers in Hawaii are called liquid sunshine.

_____ 10. The jury exonerated him, and he was imprisoned for life.

_____ 11. She felt no malice toward the person who had been hired to replace her.

_____ 12. He had recently contracted a congenital malady.

EXERCISE 3 Be sure to write in your journal each day some sentences using new words you have learned.

MORPH—form

MORPH meaning *form* is an easy root to spot and will help clarify some difficult words. For example, **amorphous** [A without + MORPH form] refers to something that is without *form*, such as a speech that has not yet been organized, a poem that is still in an unformed state, a plan that has not yet taken shape, or some clay that is ready for the potter's wheel.

amorphous (uh mawr′ fus) [A without + MORPH form]—without definite form or shape. *His notes for his lecture were still in an amorphous state, without any plan or organization.*

metamorphosis (met uh mawr′ fuh sis) [META change + MORPH form] —change of form or shape. *A caterpillar undergoes a metamorphosis when it turns into a butterfly.*

Morpheus (mawr′ fē us)—in Greek mythology the god of dreams and of the forms that dreaming sleepers see. *Morpheus was so named because of the forms he controlled in people's dreams.*

morphine (mawr′ fēn)—a drug used to bring sleep or ease pain (named after Morpheus). *The doctor prescribed morphine for the agonizing pain.*

morphology (mawr fol′ uh jē) [MORPH form + -LOGY study of]—the branch of biology that makes a study of the form of animals or plants. *The professor specializes in the morphology of frogs.*

endomorphic (en duh mawr′ fik) [ENDO inside + MORPH form]—characterized by prominence of the abdomen and other soft body parts developed from the inside layer of the embryo. *An endomorphic person has a constant struggle against becoming overweight.*

ectomorphic (ek tuh mawr′ fik) [ECTO outside + MORPH form]—characterized by a slender physical build and by prominence of structures such as skin, nerves, sense organs, and brain, developed from the outside layer of the embryo. *With his ectomorphic build, he was never able to compete in football.*

mesomorphic (mez uh mawr′ fik) [MESO middle + MORPH form]—characterized by muscular or athletic build and by prominence of bone, muscle, and connective tissue developed from the middle layer of the embryo. *The mesomorphic person tends to be successful in contact sports.*

ALSO: anthropomorphic, anthropomorphism

EXERCISE 1   Write the appropriate MORPH word.

1. She is the _____ type, muscular and good in sports.

2. He was studying _____, especially the forms of ferns.

3. _____ is a drug named after Morpheus, the god of dreams and the forms in dreams.

4. With her _____ build, she tends to put on weight.

5. An artist begins a sculpture with an _____ piece of clay.

6. My cousin is the _____ type, slender in build.

7. We observed the _____ of the tadpole into a frog.

EXERCISE 2   REVIEW   Write C in front of each sentence in which all words are used correctly.

_____   1. I tried to efface from my mind that unpleasant scene.

_____   2. The choir left the church after the malediction.

_____   3. Many cities saw the exodus of people from the inner city to the suburbs.

_____   4. The practice of monogamy is prohibited in the United States.

_____   5. The speaker was aware of the malevolent glances of his opponents.

_____   6. Generic foods are usually more expensive than brand name foods.

_____   7. We marveled at how the ancients had moved the monoliths at Stonehenge.

_____   8. Eventually we will have to think in kilometers rather than in miles.

_____   9. Her handling of the problem was so maladroit that everyone was pleased.

_____ 10. Taking away a tribe's way of getting food is really genocide.

EXERCISE 3   REVIEW   What name would you apply to a person

1. who deals in old rare books? _____

2. who studies the development and behavior of human beings? _____

3. who denies the existence of God? _____

4. who loves people and gives money to benefit them? _____

5. who disagrees with the government? _____

PAN—all

In his epic poem *Paradise Lost,* John Milton calls the capital of hell Pandemonium (PAN all + DAIMON demon), the home of *all* demons, a place of wild confusion and noise. Today **pandemonium** has come to mean any wild uproar or tumult.

Pan-American (pan uh mer′ uh kun)—including all of America, both North and South. *He hopes to participate in the Pan-American games.*

panchromatic (pan krō mat′ ik) [PAN all + CHROM color]—sensitive to light of all colors. *The panchromatic film gave him excellent pictures.*

pantomime (pan′ tuh mīm) [PAN all + MIM to imitate]—a theatrical performance in which an actor plays all the parts with gestures and without speaking. *Marcel Marceau has turned the ancient dramatic form of pantomime into an art.*

panorama (pan uh ram′ uh)—a view in all directions. *The panorama from the top of the gorge was awe-inspiring.*

pandemonium (pan duh mō′ nē um) [PAN all + DAIMON demon]—the home of all demons in Milton's *Paradise Lost*; a wild uproar. *When the winning team returned, there was pandemonium.*

panacea (pan uh sē′ uh)—a remedy for all ills or difficulties. *People who join cults are often looking for a panacea for all their troubles.*

pantheism (pan′ thē iz um) [PAN all + THE god]—the doctrine that God is all the laws and forces of nature and the universe. *He turned from the formal religions to a belief in pantheism.* Also, the ancient belief in and worship of all gods. *Pantheism was the religion of early Rome.*

pantheon (pan′ thē on) [PAN all + THE god]—a temple of all the gods. *They visited the Pantheon in Rome.* Also, the place of the idols of any group, or the idols themselves. *Eric Heiden has joined the pantheon of American Olympic heroes.*

panegyric (pan uh jir′ ik) [PAN all + AGYRIS assembly]—originally, a speech for a general assembly; now, a formal speech or writing giving extravagant praise. *The speaker delivered a panegyric about the achievements of the athletes.*

panoply (pan′ uh plē) [PAN all + HOPLON armor]—a full suit of armor; ceremonial attire; any magnificent or impressive array. *The woods in their full panoply of autumn foliage were an invitation to photographers.*

ALSO: pandemic

EXERCISE 1   Write the appropriate PAN word.

1. If you invite 20 five-year-olds to a birthday party, you'd better be prepared

   for _____.

2. The patent medicine was supposed to be a _____ for all
   diseases.

3. His love of nature and reverence for natural laws was almost _____.

4. It is worth climbing to the top of the cathedral to see the _____
   of the city.

5. _____ by a good actor can be as effective as dialogue.

6. The marching band and the pompom girls were out on the field in full

   _____.

7. The chairperson's introduction turned into a _____ about
   the lecturer's accomplishments.

8. His goal was to make the _____ of famous tennis players.

9. They used _____ film for all their pictures of the Grand
   Canyon.

EXERCISE 2   REVIEW   Write C in front of each sentence in which all words
are used correctly.

_____ 1. Children in bulky snowsuits sliding down a hill look like amorphous
          bundles.

_____ 2. The conductor was looking for a monotone to complete the bass
          section of the choir.

_____ 3. Because my car wouldn't start, my only recourse was to phone for
          a tow truck.

_____ 4. She was interested in genealogy and was listing all her nineteenth-
          century progeny.

_____ 5. The circumspect approach of the diplomat proved effective in the
          delicate negotiations.

_____ 6. The mayor was a demagogue who worked unselfishly for his con-
          stituents.

_____ 7. In high school I learned the chronology of the terms of office of the
          last eight presidents of the United States.

PATH—feeling, suffering

Do you feel sympathy or empathy when the boy on stage has forgotten his speech? And do you feel apathy or antipathy toward the ideas a lecturer is presenting?

All four words—sympathy, empathy, apathy, and antipathy—describe *feelings* because they all contain the root PATH *feeling*. **Sympathy** [SYM together + PATH feeling] is literally *feeling* together with someone. **Empathy** [EM in + PATH feeling] is a stronger word, indicating that you identify with someone so closely that you *feel* "in" that person's position. **Apathy** [A without + PATH feeling] means lack of *feeling*, indifference. **Antipathy** [ANTI against + PATH feeling] means a *feeling* against someone or something, a strong dislike.

You will of course feel sympathy for the boy who is having stage fright, and if he happens to be your child, you will certainly feel empathy—identifying with him and participating in his suffering. As for the ideas presented by a lecturer, if you disagree with them, you'll feel antipathy toward them, but if they simply don't interest you, then you'll feel only apathy. You'll be without *feeling*, **apathetic.**

sympathy (sim′ puh thē) [SYM together + PATH feeling]—*lit.* a feeling together with someone or something; a feeling for another person. *No one had any sympathy for the criminal.*

empathy (em′ puh thē) [EM in + PATH feeling]—*lit.* a feeling as if one were in the other person's place; an understanding so intimate that one participates in another's feelings. *Because he had been unemployed the year before, he now felt empathy for his unemployed friend.*

apathy (ap′ uh thē) [A without + PATH feeling]—a lack of feeling; indifference. *Voter apathy was to blame for the poor turnout on election day.*

apathetic (ap uh thet′ ik) [A without + PATH feeling]—without feeling; indifferent. *When she failed to get a promotion, she became apathetic about her job and no longer did her best.*

antipathy (an tip′ uh thē) (ANTI against + PATH feeling]—a feeling against someone or something; a strong dislike. *His antipathy toward those who disagreed with him was obvious.*

pathetic (puh thet′ ik)—arousing feelings of pity. *Seeing the dog hunt for her missing pups was pathetic.*

pathos (pā′ thos)—a quality, especially in literature, that arouses feelings of pity. *My sister loves stories full of pathos, stories she can cry over.*

psychopathic (sī kō path′ ik) [PSYCH mind + PATH suffering]—*lit.* suffering in the mind; mentally disordered. *The search for the psychopathic killer ended finally in his capture.*

pathology (pa thol′ uh jē) [PATH suffering + -LOGY study of]—*lit.* the study of suffering; the scientific study of the nature of disease, especially the structural and functional changes caused by disease. *The doctor preferred to do laboratory research in pathology rather than to treat patients.*

pathological (path uh loj′ i kul)—caused by disease. *It was finally determined that her inability to concentrate was pathological.* Also, disordered in behavior. *He was a pathological liar.*

pathogenic (path uh jen′ ik) [PATH suffering + GEN birth]—producing (giving birth to) suffering or disease. *Continual worry about health can be pathogenic.*

ALSO: telepathy

EXERCISE 1   Write the appropriate PATH word.

1. His yawn indicated his _____.

2. She feels such _____ for her son in his struggle to make the team that it's almost as if she were trying to make it herself.

3. The patient became _____ and was sent to a mental hospital.

4. My father has an _____ toward artificial flowers.

5. Her abnormal distrust of everyone was obviously _____.

6. The _____ in that movie led to a lot of sniffles.

7. With her frail health, her hectic life-style might well turn out to be

   _____.

8. The _____ report showed no abnormalities.

9. He's lost interest and has become so _____ that he doesn't care whether he ever sees her again.

PED—foot (For the PED root meaning "child" see p. 166.)

Two words containing PED were originally concerned with getting one's foot in an entanglement. **Impede** [IM in + PED foot] meant to get one's *foot* into an entanglement and thus hinder one's progress. Through the years it has lost the meaning of the foot in an entanglement and now has come to mean merely to hinder the progress of. **Expedite** [EX out + PED foot] originally meant to get one's *foot* out of an entanglement and thus to speed up one's progress. Expedite too has lost the meaning of the foot in an entanglement and today means merely to speed the progress of, to help along. You might say that a poor vocabulary will impede your progress in college whereas a large vocabulary will expedite your progress by helping you read with more understanding.

pedestrian—one who goes on foot; also, commonplace or dull, as a pedestrian style of writing

pedal—a lever operated by the foot

pedestal—a support (foot) or base, as for a column or statue

pedicure [PED foot + CUR care]—the care of the feet and toenails

quadruped (kwahd′ roo ped) [QUADR four + PED foot]—a four-footed animal. *Most mammals are quadrupeds.*

centipede (sen′ tuh pēd) [CENT hundred + PED foot]—a wormlike invertebrate popularly supposed to have a hundred feet. *In the tropics, centipedes invaded our cottage.*

pedigree (ped′ uh grē) [from the French PIED foot + DE of + GRUE crane]—*lit.* the foot of a crane, so called because the three-line diagram used to indicate descent looks like a crane's foot; a record of ancestry. *The collie's pedigree made him a valuable show dog.*

impede (im pēd′) [IM in + PED foot]—*lit.* to get the foot in an entanglement; to hinder the progress of. *An inability to read rapidly may impede one's academic progress.*

impediment (im ped′ uh munt) [IM in + PED foot]—*lit.* entanglement of the foot; anything that hinders. *The famous Greek orator Demosthenes had to overcome a speech impediment.*

expedite (ek′ spuh dīt) (EX out + PED foot]—*lit.* to get the foot out of an entanglement; to speed the progress of; to help along. *To expedite your registration, fill out the forms ahead of time.*

expedition (ek spuh dish′ un) [EX out + PED foot]—*lit.* freeing the foot; a journey for a definite purpose. *The expedition to the North Pole brought back much scientific information.*

expedient (ek spē′ dē unt) [EX out + PED foot]—*lit.* foot out of an entanglement; advantageous; useful in getting a desired result. *It might be
expedient to appoint someone who has influence with the management.*

ALSO: biped, impedimenta, pedometer

EXERCISE 1   Write the appropriate PED word.

1. Reading my reference materials ahead of time will _____
   my progress in writing my paper.
2. He was less interested in giving an honest answer than in giving an

   _____ one.
3. Spraining his ankle early in the season is going to _____
   his progress toward the championship.
4. She couldn't imagine anyone wanting a dog without a _____.

5. His unpopular voting record is an _____ in his reelec-
   tion campaign.

EXERCISE 2   REVIEW   Underline the appropriate word.

1. I'm tired of cold winters and am looking for an (equable, equitable) climate.
2. He invented an (ingenuous, ingenious) device for keeping coat hangers
   apart.
3. The backers of the bill were (ebullient, disconsolate) when it passed.
4. He and his wife weren't troubled by the (diversion, disparity) in their
   salaries.
5. The perimeter of a property is the distance (across, around) it.
6. Her poetry was (euphonious, equivocal) and pleasant to listen to.

EXERCISE 3   In your journal list two things that have impeded your progress
in mastering the words in this book and two things that have expedited your
progress.

PHIL—to love

A word containing PHIL will have something to do with *love*. Philosophy [PHIL to love + SOPH wise] is the *love* of wisdom. A **bibliophile** [BIBL book + PHIL to love] is one who *loves* books. And a **philanthropist** [PHIL to love + ANTHROP human] is one who *loves* human beings, particularly one who gives money to benefit humanity (see p. 20).

philosophy (fi los' uh fē) [PHIL to love + SOPH wise]—the love and pursuit of wisdom through reasoning. *Socrates valued philosophy more than anything else.*

philosopher (fi los' uh fur) [PHIL to love + SOPH wise]—one who loves and pursues wisdom through reasoning. *Immanuel Kant was one of the great philosophers of the eighteenth century.*

philharmonic (fil hahr mon' ik) [PHIL to love + HARMONIA harmony]— *lit.* loving harmony; devoted to music. *That winter we heard the New York Philharmonic Orchestra.*

philatelist (fi lat' uh list) [PHIL to love + ATELEIA tax exemption (the stamp showed that the postage had been prepaid, and the receiver was exempted from further charge)]—one who loves stamps; a stamp collector. *As a philatelist, she was interested in collecting flower stamps.*

bibliophile (bib' lē uh fil) [BIBL book + PHIL to love]—one who loves books; a book collector. *We discovered a small bookstore owned by a true bibliophile.*

Anglophile (ang' gluh fil) [ANGL English + PHIL to love]—one who greatly admires England, its customs, and its people. *A confirmed Anglophile, she spends every summer in England.*

philodendron (fil uh den' drun) [PHIL to love + DENDR tree]—*lit.* loving trees; a tropical climbing plant that likes the shade of trees. *She cultivated philodendron plants for their showy heart-shaped leaves.*

ALSO: Philadelphia, philanthropist, philanthropy, Philip, philippic, philology

EXERCISE 1 REVIEW Underline the appropriate word.

1. The study of the forms of animals and plants is called (morphology, pathology).

2. Her study of (entomology, etymology) had given her considerable knowledge about the history of words.

3. The company was (monolithic, amorphous), with a strong central office and many branches.

4. The course in (calligraphy, topography) improved his penmanship.

5. The cashier was accused of (malapropism, malfeasance).

6. She felt (perfidy, antipathy) toward the course, hating every moment of it.

7. The actor used (pantomime, pantheism) rather than words to present the character.

8. An interest in word roots will (impede, expedite) your learning new words.

9. The supervisor found the employee guilty of one lie after another and branded him (maladroit, perfidious).

10. A person of slender physical build is (ectomorphic, endomorphic).

11. His name was added to the (panoply, pantheon) of famous runners.

12. The 1980 census gave a valuable (genealogical, demographic) picture of the United States.

13. The census has brought about a more (equable, equitable) distribution of government funds.

14. He took the picture with a (panchromatic, philharmonic) film.

15. The (philanthropist, philatelist) showed us his collection of stamps.

EXERCISE 2 As a review of some of the roots you have learned, try to make a root chain similar to the one on page 2. Start with a word like *autobiography* or *geology*, and refer to the preceding pages to find the words you need.

PHOB—fear

Do you refuse to stand on the observation platform of a tall building? If so, perhaps you have **acrophobia,** an excessive *fear* of high places. Do you avoid elevators? If so, you may be suffering from **claustrophobia,** an excessive *fear* of closed places.

phobia (fō′ bē uh)—an excessive or illogical fear of some particular thing or situation. *Her fear of dogs has really become a phobia.*

phobic (fō′ bik)— excessively fearful. *She has a phobic desire to avoid large crowds.*

acrophobia (ak ruh fō′ bē uh) [ACRO high + PHOB fear]—an excessive or illogical fear of high places. *Because of her acrophobia, she refused to approach the rim of the canyon.*

claustrophobia (klos truh fō′ bē uh) [CLAUS to close + PHOB fear]—an excessive or illogical fear of enclosed places. *His claustrophobia made him prefer the stairs to the elevator.*

hydrophobia (hi druh fō′ bē uh) [HYDR water + PHOB fear]—an abnormal fear of water. Also, rabies (rabies was first called hydrophobia because victims were unable to swallow water). *There was an outbreak of hydrophobia among the dogs of the area.*

photophobia (fo tuh fō′ bē uh) [PHOT light + PHOB fear]—an abnormal intolerance of light. *Because of photophobia, he had to wear tinted glasses.*

xenophobia (zen uh fō′ bē uh) [XENO foreigner + PHOB fear]—fear or hatred of foreigners or strangers. *Extreme patriotism may turn into xenophobia.*

technophobia (tek nuh fō′ bē uh) [TECHN skill + PHOB fear]—lit. a fear of technology; computer anxiety. *She finally overcame her technophobia and completed a course called "Introduction to BASIC."*

EXERCISE 1 Write the appropriate PHOB word.

1. His eye problems were diagnosed as _____.

2. Because of his _____ dread of failing, he was constantly uneasy.

3. Their lack of understanding of foreigners amounted to _____.

4. She claimed she got _____ from working in a small room with no windows.

5. Wild rabbits can sometimes be the carriers of _____.

6. Going out on the high balcony bothered him because he suffered from

_____.

7. A severe attack of _____ made her decide to keep her old manual typewriter.

EXERCISE 2   REVIEW   Give the meaning of each root and a word in which it is found.

	MEANING	**WORD**
1. DICT		
2. DIS, DI, DIF		
3. EQU		
4. EU		
5. EX, ES, E		
6. FID		
7. GEN		
8. GRAPH, GRAM		
9. LOG		
10. -LOGY		
11. LOQU, LOC		
12. MAL		
13. METER, METR		
14. MIT, MIS, MISS		
15. MONO		
16. MORPH		
17. PAN		
18. PATH		
19. PED		
20. PHIL		
21. PHOB		

PHON—sound

Any word containing PHON always has something to do with *sound*. A **symphony** [SYM together + PHON sound] is literally *sounds* together, presumably pleasant sounds. If a *sound* is harsh or unpleasant, it is called **cacophony** [CACO bad + PHON sound] whereas smooth and harmonious *sounds*, especially words or phrases that please the ear, are called **euphony** [EU good + PHON sound] (see p. 54).

> **symphony** (SYM together + PHON sound]—*lit.* sounds together; an orchestra; music written for an orchestra
> **microphone** [MICRO small + PHON sound]—an instrument for intensifying weak (small) sounds
> **saxophone** [SAX (the name of the inventor) + PHON sound]—a wind instrument
> **phonograph** [PHON sound + GRAPH to write]—a machine for playing recorded (written on a disk) sounds

megaphone (meg′ uh fōn) [MEGA large + PHON sound]—*lit.* large sound; a cone-shaped device for making the sound of the voice greater. *The cheerleaders all had megaphones.*

cacophony (ka kof′ uh nē) [KAKOS bad + PHON sound]—*lit.* bad sounds; disagreeable or discordant sounds. *Only a mother can enjoy the cacophony of her child's violin practice.*

polyphonic (pol ē fon′ ik) [POLY many + PHON sound]—having two or more independent melodies all harmonizing. *A polyphonic composition has two or more melodies combined.*

stereophonic (ster ē ō fon′ ik) [STEREO solid + PHON sound]—*lit.* solid sound; giving a three-dimensional effect to sound. *A stereophonic record sounds like live music because it contains two sound tracks to make the music seem to be all around one.*

phonetics (fuh net′ iks)—the branch of language study dealing with speech sounds and their symbols. *A knowledge of phonetic symbols is an aid in learning to speak a new language.*

phonics (fon′ iks)—the use of the sounds of letters and groups of letters in teaching beginners to read. *The phonics method used to be the main method for teaching children to read.*

ALSO: antiphonal, euphonious, euphony, telephone

EXERCISE 1   Write the appropriate PHON word.

1. It was good to get out of the _____ of the office with its typewriters clacking, phones ringing, and people chattering.

2. The several melodies are combined into an unusual _____ composition.

3. The _____ was named after its inventor, Adolphe Sax.

4. Even if I used a _____, I doubt if anyone would hear what I'm trying to say.

5. His knowledge of _____ helped him pronounce French words correctly.

6. The _____ method of teaching children to read has been criticized lately because our speech sounds are so inconsistent.

EXERCISE 2   REVIEW   Write C in front of each sentence in which all words are used correctly.

_____ 1. The common cold is pandemic.

_____ 2. The demise of the old regime brought new opportunities for the youth of the country.

_____ 3. I won't let anything impede my progress in learning new words.

_____ 4. Anyone with acrophobia will not want to go into the cave.

_____ 5. An emissary brought greetings from his country.

_____ 6. It is not only philatelists who like the new commemorative stamps.

_____ 7. Only a bibliophile would be interested in that tattered old book.

_____ 8. The two countries agreed that each would quit dropping missives on the other country.

_____ 9. Her inability to sit still for even a few moments was diagnosed as pathological.

EXERCISE 3   In your journal write some sentences about cacophony.

POST—after

Preposterous is made up of PRE *before* and POST *after* and originally meant having the before part where the after part should be, as a horse with its head where its tail should be. Such a *before-after* animal would be preposterous or absurd. And so today anything contrary to nature, reason, or common sense is called preposterous.

postdate—to date a check or other document with a future date rather than the actual date

postscript [POST after + SCRIPT to write]—a note written after the main body of a letter (abbreviated PS)

postpone [POST after + PON to put]—to put off until afterward

postnatal [POST after + NAT to be born]—occurring during the period immediately after birth

postgraduate—relating to a course of study after graduation

posterity (po ster' uh tē)—those who come after; future generations. *Posterity will determine the value of his writing.*

posterior (po stir' ē ur)—located behind (as opposed to anterior, located in front). *The posterior legs of the jackrabbit are stronger than the anterior ones.*

post meridiem (pōst muh rid' ē um) [POST after + MERIDI noon]— (abbreviated PM) after noon. *The committee will meet at 3 PM.*

postmortem (post mor' tum) [POST after + MORT death]—an examination after death; an autopsy. *The postmortem revealed the cause of his death.*

preposterous (pri pos' tur us) [PRE before + POST after]—*lit.* having the before part where the after part should be; contrary to nature, reason, or common sense; absurd. *The idea of flying to the moon was once considered preposterous.*

posthumously (pos' choo mus li)—after the death of the father, as a child born posthumously; after the death of the author, as a book published posthumously; after one's death, as an award received posthumously. *The medal of honor was awarded to him posthumously.*

Postimpressionist (pōst im presh' uh nist)—*lit.* after the Impressionists; a school of painting in France in the late nineteenth century that followed the Impressionists. *Cézanne and Matisse were Postimpressionists.*

postlude (pōst lood) [POST after + LUD to play]—a piece of music played after a church service. *The organist played a Bach fugue as a postlude.*

ALSO: postnuptial, postoperative

EXERCISE 1 Write the appropriate POST word.

1. Now that the poet is dead, some of his poems are being published

   _____.

2. Perhaps his poetry will someday be read by _____.

3. Traveling faster than sound was once considered a _____ idea.

4. The _____ of a giraffe's body is less developed than the anterior.

5. During the organ _____ the congregation left the church.

6. An entire gallery in the art museum was devoted to the works of the

   _____.

7. Because the death was unexpected, a _____ was required.

EXERCISE 2 REVIEW Underline the appropriate word.

1. With no thought of (emolument, equity), the teacher spent hours helping the immigrants.

2. He would (eulogize, excoriate) his wife for the slightest error in her cooking.

3. They talked about subjects as (disparate, dissident) as mud pies and ballet.

4. The applicant tended to (equivocate, expurgate) when his former job was mentioned.

5. I was (dismantled, disconcerted) when they excluded me from their plans.

6. A distrust of foreigners is called (technophobia, xenophobia).

7. The government was constantly threatened by the (dissidents, automatons).

EXERCISE 3 Each day be sure to write a few sentences in your vocabulary journal using some of the new words you have learned.

PRE—before

PRE at the beginning of a word always means *before* and is easy to understand in such words as **preschool, premature, prehistoric, premeditate,** and **precaution.** But sometimes the meaning is not so obvious. For example, **precocious** [PRE before + COQUERE to cook] originally meant cooked *before* time. Eventually, precocious was applied to fruits that ripened early, and today it is used to describe a person who has matured earlier than usual, particularly mentally. Children who are unusually smart for their years are said to be precocious, literally cooked *before* time.

prevent [PRE before + VEN to come]—*lit.* to come before in order to keep from happening; to hinder

prevail [PRE before + VAL to be strong]—to be strong before all others; to win, as to prevail over the other contestants

prejudge [PRE before + JUD judge]—to judge beforehand without adequate evidence

prejudice [PRE before + JUD judge]—a judgment formed beforehand without examination of the facts

precise [PRE before + CIS to cut]—*lit.* to cut off unnecessary parts beforehand; sharply defined and exact

prelude (prel' yo͞od) [PRE before + LUD to play]—an introductory piece of music; a concert piece for piano or orchestra. *She played a Chopin prelude at the recital.* Also, an introductory performance or action preceding a more important one. *The passage of that law was the prelude to further civil rights legislation.*

prerequisite (prē rek' wuh zit)—something required beforehand. *Algebra is a prerequisite for geometry.*

preamble (prē' am bul) [PRE before + AMBUL to walk]—*lit.* a walking before; a preliminary statement to a document. *Have you read the Preamble to the Constitution?*

precedent (pres' uh dunt) [PRE before + CED to go]—an act that goes before and may serve as an example for later acts. *His giving his prize to charity set a precedent that later winners followed.*

unprecedented (un pres' uh den tid) [UN not + PRE before + CED to go] —never having happened before. *The sales manager took an unprecedented step when he gave the job to a teenager.*

precocious (pri kō' shus) [PRE before + COQUERE to cook]—*lit.* cooked before time; matured earlier than usual, particularly mentally. *The child was precocious, having learned to read at four.*

precipitate (pri sip' uh tāt) [PRE before + CAPIT head]—*lit.* to dash headfirst; to hasten the occurrence of. *The scandal precipitated his ruin.*

preclude (pri klōōd′) [PRE before + CLUD to shut]—*lit.* to shut out beforehand; to make impossible by a previous action; to prevent. *His poor record with that company may preclude his getting another job.*

preeminent (prē em′ uh nunt) [PRE before + EMINERE to stand out]— standing out before all others. *Edison was preeminent among the scientists of his day.*

preponderant (pri pon′ dur unt) [PRE before + PONDER weight]—outweighing; having more power or importance. *The preponderant theme of the speakers was the future welfare of the institution.*

predilection (pred l ek′ shun) [PRE before + DILIGERE to love]—*lit.* to love before others; a preference. *Her predilection for classical music kept her from being an impartial judge in the music contest.*

presage (pri sāj′) [PRE before + SAGIRE to perceive]—to perceive beforehand; to predict. *Lack of cooperation among the employees presages trouble in the industry.*

ALSO: precede, precursor, predestination, predict, predominant, premise, preposterous, prerogative, prescient, prescribe, presentiment, preside, president, pretentious, previous

---

EXERCISE 1   Write the appropriate PRE word.

1. The bank failure was _____ by the fall in interest rates.

2. She insisted that her child was _____ rather than average.

3. The court decision set a _____ that was followed for many years.

4. I have a _____ for blue and find it hard to buy any other color.

5. His strong stand against forced retirement was _____ in that company. No one had ever taken such a stand before.

6. After publishing her research, she was considered _____ in her field.

7. The testimony of the medical doctor was _____ in the minds of the jury.

8. The early morning clouds _____ a stormy day.

9. His unwillingness to negotiate _____ any hope of a reconciliation with his boss.

10. An ability to take shorthand is a _____ for the job.

11. Her question was simply a _____ to a long explanation of her reasons for resigning.

PRO—forward, before, for, forth

Do you tend to put off unpleasant tasks until a future time? If so, you probably have a **propensity** [PRO forward + PENS to hang] (a hanging *forward* or inclination) to **procrastinate** [PRO forward + CRAS tomorrow] (to push tasks *forward* until tomorrow). When it comes to studying, many students have a propensity to procrastinate.

proclaim [PRO forth + CLAM to cry out]—to announce officially and publicly

produce [PRO forth + DUC to lead]—to lead forth; to bring forth

propel [PRO forward + PEL to push]—to push or drive forward

proceed [PRO forward + CEED to go]—to go forward

provide [PRO before + VID to see]—*lit.* to see beforehand; to get ready beforehand

provision [PRO before + VIS to see]—a seeing beforehand; a preparation for the future

pronoun—a word that stands for a noun

promotion [PRO forward + MOT to move]—a moving forward, as to a better job

provident (prov' uh dunt) [PRO before + VID to see]—*lit.* seeing beforehand; making provision for the future. *If he had been more provident, he wouldn't be in need now.*

prospectus (pruh spek' tus) [PRO forward + SPECT to look]—*lit.* a looking forward; a summary of a proposed commercial, literary, or other venture. *The prospectus made the new subdivision look inviting.*

projectile (pruh jek' tul) [PRO forward + JECT to throw]—something thrown forward by force; a missile. *The projectile just missed a populated area.*

promontory (prom' un tōr ē) [PRO forward + MONT mountain]—a high peak of land or rock (mountain) jutting forward into the sea. *From the promontory we had a view of the entire area.*

procrastinate (prō kras' tuh nāt) [PRO forward + CRAS tomorrow]—*lit.* to push forward until tomorrow; to put off doing something until a future time. *I always procrastinate about cleaning the house.*

profuse (pruh fyo͞os') [PRO forth + FUS to pour]—pouring forth freely; generous. *The mechanic was profuse in her apologies.*

profusion (pruh fyo͞o' zhun) [PRO forth + FUS to pour]—*lit.* a pouring forth; an abundance. *The profusion of wild flowers on the hill delighted us.*

proponent (pruh pō′ nunt) [PRO before + PON to put]—*lit.* one who puts something before people; one who argues in favor of something; an advocate. *A leading proponent of women's rights is speaking tonight.*

propensity (pruh pen′ suh tē) [PRO forward + PENS to hang]—*lit.* a hanging forward: a natural inclination. *He has a propensity for putting things off.*

proclivity (prō kliv′ uh tē) [PRO forward + CLIVUS slope]—*lit.* a slope forward; an inclination toward something, especially toward something objectionable. *Her proclivity to exaggerate finally led to her demotion.*

(Propensity and proclivity are close synonyms.)

protuberant (prō tōō′ bur unt) [PRO forth + TUBER swelling]—bulging. *From childhood he had been conscious of his protuberant nose.*

ALSO: improvise, proclamation, progenitor, progeny, prognosis, prognosticate, program, prologue, promise, prophet, proscribe, prospect, protracted, provocation, provoke

---

EXERCISE 1   Write the appropriate PRO word.

1. The _____ for the investment fund was tempting.

2. His _____ or _____ for wasting time may cost him his job.

3. She's a _____ of the amendment to ban disposable bottles.

4. All his children inherited his _____ ears.

5. Whenever I _____, someone always quotes the old epigram, "Don't put off until tomorrow . . . ."

6. His tardiness was always followed by a _____ of excuses.

7. We stood on the _____ and looked out over the ocean.

8. Always a _____ person, he had taken care of his family's needs before he left for the month.

9. With _____ thanks, she accepted the award.

RE—back, again

What would you do with a recalcitrant child? First you might have to figure out the meaning of **recalcitrant.** Since RE means *back* and CALC means *heel*, recalcitrant means literally kicking *back* the heels. Once used of horses and mules, it now is applied to human beings. Therefore a recalcitrant child would be one who is kicking *back*, obstinate, stubbornly rebellious.

The meanings of many words that begin with RE are simple: **return** is simply to turn *again*; **recall** is call *again*, and **reconstruct** is to construct *again.* But some words that you know well may take on an added bit of meaning when you know not only RE but the meaning of the following root as well.

recede [RE back + CED to go]—to go back, as a river recedes from its banks

receive [RE again + CAP to take]—*lit.* to take again; to take something offered

record [RE again + CORD heart]—originally, to learn by heart in order to remember again; now, to write down in order to remember

recreation [RE again + CREAT to create]—*lit.* a creating again; the refreshment of mind or body after work through some form of play or amusement

reduce [RE back + DUC to lead]—to lead back, to diminish

refer [RE back + FER to carry]—to carry back for assistance

referee [RE back + FER to carry]—one to whom questions are carried back

remit [RE back + MIT to send]—to send back, as to remit payment

report [RE back + PORT to carry]—to carry back, as to report information

reside [RE back + SID to sit]—*lit.* to sit back; to dwell, as to reside in a house

residue [RE back + SID to sit]—*lit.* that which sits back; the part that remains after part has been separated away, as the residue in the bottom of a vase

retain [RE back + TEN to hold]—to hold back or keep in one's possession

revenue [RE back + VEN to come]—money that comes back from an investment

revert [RE back + VERT to turn]—*lit.* to turn back; to return to a former habit or condition

revise [RE again + VIS to see]—to see again in order to correct errors

revive [RE again + VIV to live]—to cause to live again

recession (ri sesh′ un) [RE back + CESS to go]—a going backward. *The government feared a business recession.*

Renaissance (ren′ uh sahns) [RE again + NASC to be born]—a rebirth; the revival of classical art, literature, and learning in Europe in the fourteenth, fifteenth, and sixteenth centuries. *Michelangelo was an artist of the Renaissance.*

recluse (rek′ lōōs) [RE back + CLUS to shut]—one who lives shut back from the world. *The poet Emily Dickinson lived as a recluse in her house in Amherst.*

remiss (ri mis′) [RE back + MISS to send]—*lit.* sent back or lessened; negligent; lax in attending to duty. *I've been remiss about doing my exercises.*

remission (ri mish′ un) [RE back + MISS to send]—*lit.* a sending back; a lessening, as a remission of disease; forgiveness, as remission of sins. *He enjoyed periods of remission from his illness.*

resilience (ri zil′ yunts) [RE again + SIL to leap]—*lit.* to leap again; the ability to recover quickly from illness, change, or misfortune. *With her customary resilience, she bounced back after her long illness.*

recalcitrant (ri kal′ suh trunt) [RE back + CALC heel]—*lit.* kicking back the heels; obstinate; stubbornly rebellious. *It's useless to argue with her when she's in a recalcitrant mood.*

recant (ri kant′) [RE back + CANT to sing]—to renounce a belief formerly held, especially in a formal or public manner. *The judge chose to recant publicly his former stand on capital punishment.*

recondite (rek′ un dīt) [RE back + COND to hide]—*lit.* hidden back; not easily understood; obscure. *The professor enjoyed explaining some recondite points to his captive audience.*

redoubtable (ri dou′ tuh bul) [RE (intensive) + DOUTER to doubt]—*lit.* arousing doubt or dread; arousing fear or awe. *The candidate realized he was facing a redoubtable opponent.*

ALSO: irrevocable, rebel, recapitulate, reclaim, recourse, recur, recurrent, reflect, refractory, reject, repel, respect, retort, revoke, revolve

---

EXERCISE 1 Write the appropriate RE word.

1. I could see little value in researching such a _____ subject.

2. He had never been an unruly or _____ child.

3. Occasionally, however, he would _____ to infant behavior.

4. One needs plenty of _____ to cope with all the disappointments in that job.

5. Everyone was relieved when there was a _____ of the heat wave.

6. Living like a _____, he avoids all social contacts.

7. Realizing that she had been _____ about answering letters, she spent the evening at the typewriter.

8. The candidate has taken such a strong stand that for him to _____ would be unthinkable.

9. The proponents of the tax bill faced some _____ opposition.

EXERCISE 2 REVIEW Write C in front of each sentence in which all words are used correctly.

_____ 1. Deciding to emigrate from their homeland, they moved to Canada.

_____ 2. Federal laws are attempting to eradicate sexual discrimination.

_____ 3. It wasn't an expedient time to change our plans.

_____ 4. Her technophobia made her eager to invest in a word processor.

_____ 5. Our candidate is facing some redoubtable opposition and may not win the election.

_____ 6. You can count on his resilience, however, to help him make a comeback even if he loses.

_____ 7. We were amazed at the profusion of flowers in their garden.

_____ 8. She decided to take a course in astrology at the university.

_____ 9. The public was becoming aware of the demagoguery in the mayor's speeches.

_____ 10. Going down those steep steps, I lost my equilibrium.

_____ 11. No one has ever doubted the credibility of our governor.

_____ 12. By speaking more slowly, my brother is trying to improve his diction.

_____ 13. They had a symbiotic relationship, each working better when they worked together.

_____ 14. From the top floor of the building we could see the panorama of the entire countryside.

_____ 15. The antiquarian looked through my books but found none new enough to interest him.

_____ 16. During her months of unemployment, she made me her confident.

_____ 17. The committee was recalcitrant and refused to help with the fund-raising dinner.

_____ 18. She embroidered her monograph on all her towels.

_____ 19. The results of our research were disproportionate to the amount of time we had spent.

_____ 20. They watched the smokestack emit pollutants.

_____ 21. We read the Bible story of the exodus of the Jews from Egypt.

EXERCISE 3 REVIEW Here, taken from magazine articles, are some sentences containing words you have studied. Are you sure of the meaning of every word? For any words you don't remember, consult the Word Index on page 193.

1. Natchez boasts it is the oldest city on the Mississippi River and has the largest collection of antebellum homes and buildings in the South.
2. She [Prime Minister Margaret Thatcher] excoriated the new Labor Party leaders.
3. Concerning his first experience of weightlessness, the astronaut said, "I was in an almost euphoric condition."
4. The Shah's pursuit of his own goals had engendered opposition from the intelligentsia.
5. [Shirley MacLaine] highlights the dances' meaning with a panoply of facial expressions.
6. The Soviet news agency TASS rapped the Chinese for condoning Reagan's "militarist course."
7. The basis of Deng's philosophy is summed up in his oft quoted dictum "It doesn't matter whether a cat is black or white so long as it catches mice."
8. The human propensity to test the worthiness of a thing by seeing how well it stands up to abuse—the instinct to kick the tires of a used car—is an ancient habit.
9. The success of the government's economic programs has also given rise to unprecedented problems.
10. The result has been a flood of novel investment and savings devices. Moreover, there has grown up a cacophony of conflicting claims that is bewildering investors.

SCRIB, SCRIPT—to write

In Europe in the fifth century a monk copied a manuscript, thus becoming the first European **scribe**. Before long, entire monasteries were founded to copy scriptural and literary texts. The scribes copied the texts laboriously in black, glossy letters; then other monks illuminated the capital letters with red pigment and gold leaf. Sometimes the making of a single book would occupy many years or even the lifetime of a monk.

scribe—one who copies manuscripts

script—handwriting; also, the written copy of a play used by actors to learn their lines

scribble—to write carelessly

Scripture—originally, anything written; now, the Bible

manuscript [MANU hand + SCRIPT to write]—originally, something written by hand; now, a composition for publication

describe [DE down + SCRIBE to write]—to write down an account of

inscribe [IN in + SCRIB to write]—originally, to engrave words in stone; now, to write in, as the dedication of a book

prescribe [PRE before + SCRIB to write]—to write down a rule beforehand; in medicine, to order a treatment

subscribe [SUB under + SCRIB to write]—to write one's name at the end of (under) a document in support of it; to give approval

subscription [SUB under + SCRIB to write]—a purchase made by signing (writing) one's name under an agreement

conscription (kun skrip' shun) [CON together + SCRIPT to write]—*lit.* names written together; an enforced enrollment or military draft. *Conscription was often necessary to provide a large army.*

nondescript (non' di skript)—not easy to describe; lacking in distinctive qualities. *Even though she was wearing a nondescript outfit, she was still the most striking person in the room.*

transcribe (tran skrīb') [TRANS over + SCRIB to write]—to write over again, as to transcribe notes. *After taking dictation in shorthand, he immediately transcribed his notes at the typewriter.*

ascribe (uh skrīb') [AD to + SCRIB to write]—*lit.* to write to; to attribute. *His parents ascribed his actions to his eagerness to succeed.*

proscribe (prō skrīb') [PRO before + SCRIB to write]—in ancient Rome, to publish the name of one condemned to death; now, to condemn or forbid as harmful. *Some religions proscribe abortion.*

ALSO: circumscribe, postscript, transcript

EXERCISE 1   Write the appropriate SCRIB, SCRIPT word.

1. They will probably _____ the failure of their plan to lack of funds.
2. His clothes were always _____ and unpressed.
3. It's wise to _____ one's class notes immediately after taking them.
4. During times of peace _____ is unnecessary.
5. Do you _____ to all his new ideas?
6. The court has _____ racial discrimination in housing.

EXERCISE 2   REVIEW   Write C in front of each sentence in which all words are used correctly.

_____ 1. The Roman belief in many gods is called pantheism.

_____ 2. The proponents of the metric system are trying to bring the United States into line with the rest of the world.

_____ 3. To procrastinate about doing an unpleasant task simply postpones it.

_____ 4. The prospectus of the new development made us want to move there.

_____ 5. Because her parents had not been provident, she was never in want.

_____ 6. The Renaissance in Italy was a revolt of the common people.

_____ 7. The captain had set a precedent of fair play that his teammates now followed.

_____ 8. Raphael is my favorite Postimpressionist.

_____ 9. The choir left the church during the organ postlude.

_____ 10. Her excellent vocabulary was an impediment to her reading.

_____ 11. The child's fear of the dark has become a phobia.

_____ 12. The criminal was judged psychopathic and sent to a mental hospital.

_____ 13. The circus barker shouted through a megaphone.

_____ 14. The politician had made his statement and refused to recant.

SED, SID, SESS—to sit

If you have a **sedentary** job, you probably *sit* at a desk all day. If you work **assiduously,** you literally *sit* at your work until it is finished. And if you have an **insidious** habit, it is one that does not seem very bad at first but that *sits* in wait for you, ready to become more and more harmful.

president [PRE before + SID to sit]—*lit.* one who sits before a group as its head

preside [PRE before + SID to sit]—*lit.* to sit before a meeting to conduct it

sedan—a portable chair seating one person; a closed automobile seating four to six persons

sediment—material that sits at the bottom of a liquid, as the sediment in a stream

session—the sitting together of a group

siege—*lit.* sitting down before a town with the intention of capturing it

assess (uh ses') [AD to + SESS to sit]—*lit.* to sit near to a judge (as an assistant); to estimate the value of property for taxation. *Their property was assessed at a higher rate than formerly.*

assessor (uh ses' ur) [AD to + SESS to sit]—*lit.* one who sits near to a judge as his assistant. *They were waiting for the assessor to evaluate their new home.*

subside (sub sīd') [SUB under + SID to sit]—*lit.* to sit under; to sink to a lower level; to settle down. *After midnight the noise subsided.*

subsidy (sub' suh dē) [SUB under + SID to sit]—*lit.* sitting under prices to hold them up; government financial support. *When corn prices were low, the farmers received a subsidy.*

subsidiary (sub sid' ē er ē) [SUB under + SID to sit]—*lit.* sitting under; serving to assist or supplement; subordinate. *The company had several subsidiary branches.*

sedative (sed' uh tiv)—*lit.* a medicine that makes one sit down or quiet down; a medicine that calms nervousness or excitement. *The doctor prescribed a sedative to calm him.*

sedate (si dāt')—keeping a quiet, steady attitude as one would when sitting; calm and quiet. *The sedate young lady was always composed no matter what happened.*

sedentary (sed' n ter ē)—requiring much sitting. *Because he had a sedentary job, he didn't get enough exercise.*

obsess (ub ses') [OB against + SESS to sit]—*lit.* to sit against; to besiege like an evil spirit; to preoccupy the mind abnormally. *He was obsessed with the fear of failure.*

obsession (ub sesh' un) [OB against + SESS to sit]—originally, the act of an evil spirit in ruling (sitting against) one; now, a persistent idea, desire, or emotion that cannot be got rid of by reasoning. *Her desire to get into the movies had become an obsession.*

supersede (soo pur sēd') [SUPER above + SED to sit]—*lit.* to sit above; to take the place of; to displace. *Solar heating is superseding other forms of heating in many places.*

insidious (in sid' ē us) [IN in + SID to sit]—*lit.* sitting in wait for; treacherous; more dangerous than seems evident. *Malaria is an insidious disease, remaining in the body ready to strike again and again.*

assiduous (uh sij' oo us)—*lit.* sitting at something until it is finished; persevering. *The new clerk was assiduous in performing all his duties.*

ALSO: assiduity, dissident, reside, residue, séance

EXERCISE 1   Write the appropriate SED, SID, SESS word.

1. A _____ occupation had never appealed to her because she didn't like to sit still.

2. Nevertheless she was an _____ worker, doing the job to the best of her ability.

3. The government _____ to farmers was cut back during the depression.

4. The chemicals had an _____ effect on the stream, the real damage not showing up for months.

5. The complaints of the environmentalists about the situation did not _____ when the election was over.

6. The word processor is going to _____ the typewriter.

7. Having everything immaculate is an _____ with her.

8. Remaining perfectly _____, she ignored the uproar around her.

9. The company's _____ offices were located overseas where labor was cheaper.

10. Becoming _____ with a desire to win, he thought of nothing else.

11. What he has done for the school is so important that it would be difficult to _____ its value.

12. The county _____ evaluated their land.

SPEC, SPIC, SPECT—to look

In ancient Rome certain men were appointed to *look* at the flight of birds for omens or signs. The kind of birds, their position in the sky, and the direction of their flight determined whether the time was **auspicious** (AVI bird + SPIC to look) for any new undertaking. The term auspicious came to mean "full of good omens," and still today we speak of an auspicious time to ask a favor, to recommend a change, or to suggest a new policy.

aspect [AD to + SPECT to look]—the way something looks from a certain point of view

expect [EX out + SPECT to look]—to look out for; to wait for

inspect [IN into + SPECT to look]—to look into carefully

prospect [PRO forward + SPECT to look]—a looking forward; the outlook for something, as a prospect for a good crop

respect [RE again + SPECT to look]—*lit.* to look on again; to look on with regard or esteem

suspect [SUB under + SPECT to look]—to look under outward appearances; to distrust

species—a group of plants or animals in which one can see (look at) like characteristics; distinct kind or sort

spectacle—something remarkable to look at

spectacular—sensational to look at, as a spectacular scene; an elaborate show, as a spectacular on television

spectator—one who looks on

spectacles—lenses through which one looks at things

conspicuous [CON (intensive) + SPIC to look]—easy to notice (look at); obvious

specimen—something to look at as an example of its kind

spy—to look at secretly

speculate (spek' yuh lāt)—*lit.* to look at; to reflect on or ponder. *The candidate speculated on his chances of winning.*

perspective (pur spek' tiv) [PER through + SPECT to look]—the ability to look at things in their true relationship; point of view. *Whether you consider the difficulty insurmountable depends on your perspective.*

retrospect (ret' ruh spekt) [RETRO backward + SPECT to look]—a looking backward. *In retrospect his life did not seem so unhappy.*

introspection (in truh spek' shun) [INTRO within + SPECT to look]—a looking within one's own mind. *Introspection was valuable in helping her solve some of her problems.*

despicable (des' pi kuh bul) [DE down + SPIC to look]—looked down on; deserving to be despised; contemptible. *Reading someone else's mail is a despicable thing to do.*

spectrum (spek' trum)—a series of colored bands seen when light passes through a prism. *All the colors of the spectrum were included in her painting.* Also, a broad range of ideas or activities. *His interests included the entire spectrum of the arts.*

specter (spec' tur)—a mental image that looks real; a ghost; any object of fear or dread. *Her father was constantly troubled by the specter of unemployment.*

auspicious (aw spish' us) [AVI bird + SPIC to look]—originally, looking at the flight of birds for omens; today, promising good luck; favorable. *It wasn't an auspicious time to ask for a raise.*

specious (spē' shus)—looking good on first sight but actually not so. *It was hard not to be taken in by the specious advertising for curing baldness.*

perspicacious (per spi kā' shus) [PER through + SPIC to look]—having the ability to look through something and understand it; perceptive. *In dealing with individual employee problems, he was exceptionally perspicacious.*

ALSO: circumspect, conspicuous, inauspicious, introspective, perspicacity, prospector, prospectus, respectable, retrospection, specific, suspicious

---

EXERCISE 1   Write the appropriate SPEC, SPIC, SPECT word.

1. The failure of the first project was not an _____ start for the coming year.

2. The salesperson could see the problem from the customer's _____.

3. She enjoyed living those years again in _____.

4. He examined his motives in a moment of quiet _____.

5. Cheating the person who had befriended him was _____.

6. The professor was unusually _____ in analyzing the problems of the students.

7. The _____ advertising made the car deal look like a give-away.

8. In that play one experiences the entire _____ of emotions.

9. The _____ of failure haunted her.

SUB—under

Prisoners in Roman times were forced to crawl *under* a yoke (like the yoke put on oxen) formed from three spears, thus showing that from that time forward they were the subjects of their conquerors. They were brought *under* (SUB) the yoke (JUGUM) or **subjugated**. We still use the word subjugate today to mean subdue or make subservient.

Many SUB words are easy to understand when we know that SUB means *under*: **subcommittee, subconscious, subcontractor, subculture, subnormal, substandard,** and **subway**. But SUB can also help clarify the meaning of some less common words such as **subliminal** and **subsume**.

submit [SUB under + MIT to send]—to put (send) oneself under the authority of another

subject (accent on last syllable) [SUB under + JECT to throw]—*lit.* to throw under the influence of; to submit to the authority of, as to subject oneself to a strict diet

submerge [SUB under + MERG to plunge]—to plunge under water

subordinate [SUB under + ORDIN order]—to put in a lower or inferior order

subterranean (sub tuh rā′ nē un) [SUB under + TERR earth]—under the surface of the earth. *Subterranean remains of an early civilization were found on the island.*

subsistence (sub sis′ tunts)—*lit.* underexistence; the barest means to sustain life. *They had barely enough food for subsistence.*

subjugate (sub′ juh gāt) [SUB under + JUGUM a yoke]—*lit.* to place under a yoke; to conquer. *The invaders subjugated the primitive tribe.*

subservient (sub sur′ vē unt) [SUB under + SERV to serve]—*lit.* serving under someone; submissive, as a servant might be. *His attitude toward his superiors was always subservient.*

subterfuge (sub′ tur fyōōj) [SUB under + FUG to flee]—*lit.* fleeing under cover; an action used to avoid an unpleasant situation. *By using the subterfuge of having to work overtime, he avoided going to the meeting.*

subversive (sub vur′ siv) [SUB under + VERS to turn]—*lit.* to turn under; tending to undermine or overthrow. *The government was threatened by subversive groups.*

subpoena (suh pē′ nuh) [SUB under + POENA penalty (the first two words of the order)]—a legal order requiring a person to appear in court to give testimony. *She received a subpoena to appear in court the next week.*

subliminal (sub lim' uh nul) [SUB under + LIMIN threshold]—below the threshold of conscious perception. *The popcorn ad flashed on the theater screen too briefly to be seen consciously, but it had a subliminal effect because people immediately started going to the lobby for popcorn.*

sub rosa (sub rō' zuh) [SUB under + ROS rose]—*lit.* under the rose (from an ancient custom of hanging a rose over the council table to indicate that all present were sworn to secrecy); in confidence. *In the interview the president was speaking sub rosa.*

subsume (sub sōōm') [SUB under + SUM to take]—to include under a more general category. *The three minor rules are subsumed under the major one.*

ALSO: subaltern, subcutaneous, subjective, submarine, submit, suborn, subscribe, subsequent, subside, subsidy, subtle, suburb, suffuse, surreptitious, suspect

---

EXERCISE 1   Write the appropriate SUB word.

1. With such a low-paying job, he and his family lived at a _____ level.
2. The dictator was trying to quell the _____ forces in the country.
3. She thought of a clever _____ to get out of doing the job.
4. He was so _____ that he never objected to his supervisor's unreasonable demands.
5. The superpower was trying to _____ all the small nations around it .
6. A person can be influenced not only in conscious ways but also in

   _____ ways.
7. Actually all his other arguments can be _____ under his one main argument.
8. The driver of the other car received a _____ to appear in court as a witness.
9. Bats flew out of the _____ cave.
10. Unwilling to have his remarks published, the dean asked that they be

    considered _____.

EXERCISE 2   Add a few more words to your WORD LIST at the end of the book. Are you using your words in conversation?

SUPER—above, over

How do you describe people who raise their eyebrows and look down on others in a haughty way? Two roots—SUPER *above* and CILIUM *eyelid*—combined to form the Latin word *supercilium* meaning eyebrow. And eventually anyone who raised the eyebrows in a haughty way came to be called a **supercilious** person, a raised-eyebrows person.

superb—above ordinary quality; excellent

superfluous [SUPER over + FLU to flow]—*lit.* overflowing what is needed; extra

superior—above others

supreme—above all others; highest in rank

superstition [SUPER above + STA to stand]—*lit.* a belief standing above other beliefs; a belief that is inconsistent with the known laws of science

supervise [SUPER over + VIS to see]—to oversee others

supervisor [SUPER over + VIS to see]—one who oversees others

surplus [SUPER above + PLUS more]—*lit.* above more; above what is needed

soprano—one having a voice range above other voices

supersonic (sōō pur son′ ik) [SUPER above + SON sound]—above the speed of sound. *Supersonic planes cause the sound known as sonic boom.*

superimpose (sōō pur im pōz′)—to lay something over something else. *The modern painting had been superimposed on an old masterpiece.*

supercilious (sōō pur sil′ ē us) [SUPER above + CILIUM eyelid]—*lit.* above the eyelid; eyebrows raised in a haughty way. *She cast a supercilious glance at the person who had dared to disagree with her.*

supernumerary (sōō pur nōō′ muh rer ē [SUPER above + NUMER number]—someone in excess of (above) the number required; an extra. *Since she was given no work to do, she felt like a supernumerary.* Also, a performer in the theater without a speaking part. *He was a supernumerary in the mob scene.*

insuperable (in sōō′ pur uh bul) [IN not + SUPER over]—not capable of being overcome. *His height was an insuperable barrier to his becoming a jockey.*

ALSO: superabundant, superannuated, superhuman, superintend, supernatural, supersede

EXERCISE 1 REVIEW As a review of the words you've been studying, copy the underlined words and fill in the blanks below. How many of the ten words do you know without looking them up?

A town meeting was called to consider a lumber company's proposal to cut trees in a town-owned woodland. The proponents of the plan claimed it would create jobs and bring unprecedented wealth to the town, which was in a chronic depression. They said that those trying to circumvent the plan were asking for the demise of the community.

Those interested in ecology, on the other hand, said that the natural beauty of the area would be spoiled and that several endemic plants might become extinct. It isn't possible, they said, to equate financial gain with the good life.

The problem seemed insuperable because after three hours of discussion, no consensus was reached.

WORD	ROOT	ROOT MEANING	WORD MEANING
1.			
2.			
3.			
4.			
5.			
6.			
7.			
8.			
9.			
10.			

SYN, SYM, SYL—together, with

Among the ancient Greeks, a **symposium** was a drinking *together* party [SYM together + POS to drink], especially after a banquet. Through the years the meaning has changed until today a symposium is no longer a drinking party but a meeting or conference at which several speakers come *together* to deliver opinions on a certain topic.

We have seen that the root SYN, SYM, SYL means *together* in such words as **symmetrical, asymmetrical, sympathy, symphony,** and **synchronize.** Whether the word will begin with SYN, SYM, or SYL often depends on what letter follows. For instance, it would be difficult to pronounce SYNmetrical; therefore SYN becomes SYM, and we say SYMmetrical. For more about how a root may change one of its letters for easier pronunciation, see page 6.

synopsis [SYN together + OP sight]—*lit.* a seeing things together; a brief general summary

symbol [SYM together + BOL to throw]—*lit.* things thrown together for comparison; something that represents something else, as diamonds are a symbol of wealth

synagogue [SYN together + AGOG to lead]—a place where Jewish people are led together for worship

synthetic (sin thet' ik) [SYN together + THET to put]—*lit.* put together; produced by putting separate elements together; artificial. *Instead of a synthetic cloth, she wanted a natural fiber such as silk or cotton.*

synthesis (sin' thuh sis) [SYN together + THES to put]—*lit.* a putting together; the combining of separate elements into a whole. *Sandburg said that poetry is a synthesis of hyacinths and biscuits.*

syndrome (sin' drōm) [SYN together + DROM to run]—*lit.* a running together; a group of symptoms that run together and indicate a specific disease or condition. *He had the usual flu syndrome: sore throat, headache, and aching muscles.*

synod (sin' ud) [SYN together + OD road, journey]—*lit.* a journey together; a council or assembly, especially of church officials. *The church synod met in a different city each year.*

syntax (sin' tax) [SYN together + TAX arrangement]—the way words are arranged together to form sentences. *Because English was a second language for her, she often had trouble with syntax.* Also, in computer science, the rules governing the construction of any computer language. *The computer kept responding, "Syntax error."*

symposium (sim pō′ zē um) [SYM together + POS to drink]—originally, a drinking (together) party following a banquet among the early Greeks; now, a meeting at which several speakers deliver opinions on a certain topic. *A symposium on the use of national parks was held in Washington, D.C.*

synergistic (sin ur jis′ tik) [SYN together + ERG work]—working together, as when the joint action of two drugs increases the effectiveness of each. *Certain drugs when taken together are synergistic. The two playwrights had a synergistic relationship, each working more effectively when they worked together.*

syllogism (sil′ uh jiz um) [SYL together + LOG word]—*lit.* words together; a form of argument or reasoning consisting of two statements and a conclusion drawn from them. *Here is an example of a syllogism: All mammals are warm-blooded; whales are mammals; therefore whales are warm-blooded.*

ALSO: asymmetric, photosynthesis, symbiosis, symbiotic, symmetrical, sympathy, symphony, synchronize, synergy, synonym

---

EXERCISE 1   Write the appropriate SYN, SYM, SYL word.

1. The final motion was a _____ of all their ideas.

2. Six speakers were scheduled for the _____ on air pollution.

3. _____ cloth is made by combining various chemical elements.

4. The diagnosis was simple because the child had the typical chicken pox

   _____.

5. The matter was discussed at the annual meeting of the church _____.

6. Because he had never paid any attention to grammar in high school, he

   now had difficulty using correct _____ in his writing.

7. Learning the correct form for a _____ helped her to think logically.

8. She and her husband had a _____ relationship, each working better on the project when they worked together.

9. In an early chapter of *The Grapes of Wrath*, Steinbeck uses a turtle as a

   _____ of the migrants.

EXERCISE 2   Each day be sure to write a few sentences in your vocabulary journal using some of the new words you have learned.

TELE—far

Any word containing TELE will have *far* in its meaning. Such words as **telephone** and **telegraph** and **television** have become so common that we say them without thinking what they really mean.

telephone [TELE far + PHON sound]—an instrument for transmitting sounds from far away

telegraph [TELE far + GRAPH to write]—*lit.* an instrument for far writing; a system for transmitting messages by electric impulses sent through a wire or converted into radio waves

television [TELE far + VIS to see]—an instrument for seeing images from afar

telescope [TELE far + SCOP to look]—an instrument for looking at far objects

telecommunication—the transmission or reception of signals, writing, sounds, or intelligence of any nature by wire, radio, light beam, or any other electromagnetic means

teletypewriter (tel uh tīp′ rī tur)—an electromechanical typewriter that sends or receives messages carried by telegraph wires. *The news came to the newspaper office by Teletype.*

telex (tel′ eks)—a communication system consisting of teletypewriters connected to a telephonic network to send and receive messages. *The word* telex *is made from the first three letters of* teletypewriter *and the first two letters of* exchange.

Telstar (tel′ stahr)—*lit.* far star; a satellite for global communication put in orbit in 1962. *Telstar transmits television pictures and telephone messages.*

telepathy (tuh lep′ uh thē) [TELE far + PATH feeling]—*lit.* far feeling; the supposed communication between two people far apart by other than normal sensory means. *Because they so often thought of the same thing at the same time, they were convinced it was telepathy.*

telemetry (tuh lem′ uh trē) [TELE far + METER measure]—the automatic measurement and transmission of data by radio from far away, as from space vehicles to a receiving station. *Reports of the weather on Mars came to the research center in California by telemetry.*

ALSO: telegram, telephoto

EXERCISE 1 REVIEW Write C in front of each sentence in which all words are used correctly.

_____ 1. The flood subsided before too much damage was done.

_____ 2. In retrospect she realized how many wrong decisions she had made.

_____ 3. We are looking for a specious house, one with at least ten rooms.

_____ 4. Someone had superimposed an old masterpiece on a modern painting.

_____ 5. We found that the problem was insuperable and could easily be solved with a little effort.

_____ 6. Leaving the job half finished was a despicable thing to do.

_____ 7. He received his pedigree at the spring convocation.

_____ 8. The specter of unemployment haunted the entire town.

_____ 9. She has a propensity to talk when she should be working.

_____ 10. The director tried to influence the board members, but they were recalcitrant.

_____ 11. He ascribed his success to hard work and a bit of luck.

_____ 12. The candidate was assiduous in canvassing every house in the district.

_____ 13. The hostess cast a supercilious glance at the guest who arrived in jeans.

_____ 14. The police were on a tour of introspection in the neighborhood.

_____ 15. To proscribe is to write a prescription for medicine.

_____ 16. A postmortem examination and an autopsy are the same thing.

_____ 17. Remiss means to miss again.

_____ 18. The people in the developing country had only enough food for subsistence.

_____ 19. The old manuscript had been copied and illustrated by scribes.

_____ 20. She took a sedative to get some extra energy.

_____ 21. All my arguments can be subsumed under one main argument.

_____ 22. His saving paper in order to save trees has become an obsession.

_____ 23. For the mob scene in the movie, hundreds of supernumeraries were hired.

_____ 24. They walked over to the syndrome to watch the football practice.

_____ 25. The microwave oven will eventually supersede the conventional oven.

TORT—to twist

If you are driving along a little-traveled mountain road, you will certainly understand the meaning of **tortuous**. It comes from the root TORT *to twist* and means full of *twists* and turns. You can speak of a tortuous road, a tortuous path through the woods, a tortuous climb down a mountain, a tortuous career with advances and reverses all along the way, or tortuous arguments that wander all over rather than moving directly toward a goal. Tortuous may also mean morally *twisted*, deceitful, not straightforward. Tortuous explanations may *twist* the truth, and tortuous deals may be a little *twisted* or crooked.

Tortuous must not be confused with **torturous,** which is related to torture and means inflicting physical or mental pain.

torture—originally, a twisting of a victim's arms and legs on the rack; now, any severe physical or mental pain

retort [RE back + TORT to twist]—*lit.* a twisting back on the giver; a reply to an insult or criticism

distort [DIS away + TORT to twist]—*lit.* to twist away; to twist from the true meaning, as to distort the facts

torment—*lit.* to twist; to annoy

torch—a portable light produced by a flammable material twisted around the end of a stick and ignited (early torches were made of twisted flax dipped in tallow.)

extort (ek stawrt') [EX out + TORT to twist]—*lit.* to twist something out; to obtain by violence or threat. *They tried to extort money by blackmail.*

tortoise (tawr' tus)—a turtle, especially a land turtle, so called perhaps because of its twisted feet. *The waitress worked at the speed of a tortoise.*

contortionist (kun tawr' shun ist) [CON together + TORT to twist]—an acrobat who can twist the body and limbs into extraordinary positions. *At the circus we watched an expert contortionist.*

torturous (tawr' chur us)—inflicting physical or mental pain. *The defendant had to undergo torturous questioning.*

tortuous (tawr' chū us)—full of twists and turns. *Drive cautiously because that's a tortuous road.* Also, not straightforward; deceitful. *Her tortuous dealings gave her the reputation of being untrustworthy.*

tort (tawrt)—*lit.* a twisted action; a wrongful act, injury, or damage for which a civil suit can be brought for damages. *If a person breaks a shop window, that person has committed a tort against the shop owner.*

nasturtium (nuh stur' shum) [NAS nose + TORT to twist]—*lit.* nose twister (from the sharp odor of the plant); a plant having yellow or orange flowers and a pungent odor. *The leaves and seeds of the nasturtium are sometimes used as seasoning.*

ALSO: contortion, torque, torsion

EXERCISE 1 Write the appropriate TORT word.

1. By threatening to resign she tried to _____ a promise of promotion.
2. With a clever _____ to the insult, he managed to change the subject.
3. The audience was amazed at the acrobatic performance of the _____.
4. Emphasizing unimportant details, she tried to _____ the case.
5. The judge branded the defendant's questionable dealings with the loan company as _____.
6. I spent a _____ morning having a wisdom tooth pulled.
7. The civil suit regarding that _____ was settled out of court.

EXERCISE 2 REVIEW Write C in front of each sentence in which all words are used correctly.

_____ 1. The small nation refused to be subjugated by its powerful neighbor.
_____ 2. Although she did not appear ill, her friends knew she was suffering from an insidious disease.
_____ 3. By a clever subterfuge, he avoided taking part in the television debate.
_____ 4. Her proclivity toward revealing trade secrets cost her her job.
_____ 5. The subpoena released him from jail.
_____ 6. Utterly ingenuous, he never realized that the report might be a hoax.
_____ 7. She was malignant when she heard that she had been fired.
_____ 8. Always a sedate person, she kicked off her shoes and sat down on the floor.
_____ 9. The apathy of the committee precluded their accomplishing much.
_____ 10. Preeminent in her field, she was also knowledgeable in several others.
_____ 11. Most of the work in that company is done not in the main office but in the subsidiary offices.

TRI—three

Like UNI (one) and BI (two), TRI is easy to spot at the beginning of many words, but knowing the roots that follow often gives the words new meaning. And sometimes a TRI word has a long history. For example, **tribe** originally referred to one of the *three* groups into which the Roman people were divided.

trio—any three people or things joined or associated

triplets—three children born at one birth

triangle—a plane figure having three sides and three angles

tribe—originally, one of the three groups into which the Romans were divided; now, a group of people united by the same race and customs

tripod [TRI three + POD foot]—a three-legged stand for supporting a camera or other instrument

triplicate (trip′ li kit) [TRI three + PLIC to fold]—threefold; one of three identical copies or things. *The boss asked for the letters in triplicate.*

triennial (trī en′ ē ul) [TRI three + ENN year]—occurring every three years. *The society held a triennial convention.*

trilingual (tri ling′ gwul) [TRI three + LINGU language]—speaking three languages. *In Switzerland many people are trilingual, speaking German, French, and Italian.*

trilateral (trī lat′ ur ul) [TRI three + LATER side]—having three sides. *The three countries signed a trilateral treaty.*

tripartite (trī pahr′ tīt)—composed of three parts; shared by three parties. *The three countries made a tripartite agreement.*

(Trilateral and tripartite are close synonyms.)

trinity (trin′ uh tē)—a set of three persons or things that form a unit, as the three divine persons of Christian theology. *The Apostles' Creed affirms belief in the Trinity.*

trilogy (tril′ uh jē)—three literary, dramatic, or musical compositions that, though each is complete in itself, make a related series. *Last year I read all three books of Tolkien's trilogy The Lord of the Rings.*

trivet (triv′ it)—a three-legged stand for holding a vessel or dish. *The vase stood on a small black trivet.*

trident trid′ unt) [TRI three + DENT tooth]—a long three-pronged (toothed) spear. *Neptune, the Roman god of the sea, is usually pictured holding a trident.*

ALSO: trigonometry, trinomial, trivia, trivial

EXERCISE 1   What TRI word names the following?

1. the three divine persons of Christian theology _____

2. a three-legged stand _____ or _____

3. a long three-pronged spear _____

4. three literary compositions in a series _____

What TRI word describes the following?

5. a person who speaks three languages _____

6. a meeting held every three years _____

7. a treaty shared by three countries _____ or _____

EXERCISE 2   REVIEW   Write C in front of each sentence in which all words are used correctly.

_____ 1. Her kitchen contained a full panoply of modern equipment.

_____ 2. The speaker was smartly dressed in a nondescript outfit.

_____ 3. His unpleasant retort may precipitate a quarrel.

_____ 4. Her path to fame had been tortuous, with many wins and many losses.

_____ 5. Living like a recluse, he enjoyed chatting with his neighbors.

_____ 6. Despite his protuberant belly, he still munches chocolate bars.

_____ 7. It was a long, torturous road down the mountain.

_____ 8. Anyone with a sedentary job is sure to get plenty of exercise.

_____ 9. Telemetry has enabled us to discover many facts about Mars.

_____ 10. The doctor was unusually perspicacious in diagnosing the illness.

_____ 11. The child was precocious but had a profusion of emotional problems.

_____ 12. The ads flashing on the screen for seconds had a subliminal effect on the viewers.

_____ 13. Their report was a synthesis of the ideas that had been presented at the symposium.

_____ 14. The director was given profuse praise by the grateful cast.

_____ 15. The two worked together in a synergistic relationship.

_____ 16. Preponderant in my mind was the necessity of saving that forest from the developers.

VER—true

If you doubt someone's **veracity**, you doubt that person's *truthfulness*. If you speak of a **veritable** downpour of rain, you mean that it was *truly* a downpour. To **verify** something is to prove that it is *true*. When jury members give a **verdict** [VER true + DICT to speak], they are literally speaking the *truth*. Even the little word **very** comes from VER and means *truly*.

> **verdict** [VER true + DICT to speak]—*lit.* a speaking of the truth; the decision of a jury
> **verify**—to prove something is true
> **very**—truly, absolutely

verification (ver ruh fuh kā′ shun)—establishment of the truth. *Before cashing the check, the clerk asked for verification of the customer's identity.*

verifiable (ver′ uh fī uh bul)—capable of being proved true. *None of his statements were verifiable.*

verily (ver′ uh lē)—an archaic word meaning truly. *"Verily, I say unto you" is a common expression in the Bible.*

veritable (ver′ uh tuh bul)—true; actual. *He was a veritable Good Samaritan.*

veracity (vuh ras′ uh tē)—truthfulness. *No one doubted her veracity.*

veracious (vuh rā′ shus)—truthful; accurate. *The newspaper gave a veracious account of the incident.*

verity (ver′ uh tē)—a statement, principle, or belief that is considered to be established truth, as religious verities. *Alone on the mountain, he had time to ponder the eternal verities.*

aver (uh vur′) [AD to + VER true]—to declare to be true; to state positively. *The witness averred that he had never seen the thief before.*

ALSO: verisimilitude

EXERCISE 1   Write the appropriate VER word.

1. With her amazing knowledge of facts, she's a _____ encyclopedia.
2. He'd never lie to you; you can depend on his _____.
3. I was careful to _____ each fact before presenting it.
4. The train conductor asked for _____ of the child's age.
5. You can count on her to give a _____ report of the trial because she always tells the truth.
6. Naturally he _____ on the witness stand that he was innocent.
7. Little _____ evidence could be obtained about the accident because there had been no witnesses.
8. He was now questioning some of the _____ he had always accepted in his youth.

EXERCISE 2   REVIEW   Underline the appropriate word.

1. Their (assiduous, insidious) tactics misled their clients.
2. My sister has a (phobic, endemic) fear of air travel.
3. The dean suspected that there were (subversive, subsistence) activities going on in the dorms.
4. They objected to the (xenophobia, cacophony) of their neighbors at all hours of the night.
5. The police (proscribed, ascribed) the accident to drunken driving.
6. The (veracity, verdict) of the witness was never questioned.
7. Those clouds (preclude, presage) a storm very soon.
8. The contestant was (assessed, obsessed) with a desire to succeed.
9. The statements in the document were not (verifiable, veritable); we had no way to find out whether they were true.
10. The vase stood on a small (trident, trivet) on the hall table.
11. She believed she could communicate with faraway friends by (telemetry, telepathy).
12. The view from the (promontory, proclivity) was inspiring.
13. The Hebrew nation practiced (monotheism, pantheism).
14. Pencils are made from (graphite, graffiti).
15. The three countries made a (tripartite, trilingual) arms agreement.
16. Because I liked the first volume, I wanted to read the rest of the (trilogy, trinity).
17. One group has a yearly meeting, and the other has a (triennial, trilateral) meeting.

VERT, VERS—to turn

A **verse** or line of poetry comes from the root VERS *to turn*. Just as a plow makes a furrow and then at the end of the furrow *turns* to make another parallel one, so a verse of poetry *turns* when it comes to the end of the line and goes back to make another line.

Universe also comes from the root VERS. It is made up of UNI *one* and VERS *to turn* and means literally all things that exist *turned* into one. The ancients thought all the heavenly bodies were *turning* around the earth, *turning* into one whole.

divert [DI away + VERT to turn]—to turn away, as to turn someone's attention away from something

advertise [AD to + VERT to turn]—to turn attention to

universe [UNI one + VERS to turn]—*lit.* all things that exist turned into one; everything in the heavens turned into one whole

verse—*lit.* turning from one line to the next in poetry, like a plow turning to make parallel furrows

version—a translation or turning of one language into another, as a version of Homer; an account related from a specific point of view, as a version of an accident

convert [CON together + VERT to turn]—*lit.* to turn together to the same belief; to turn from one belief to another

convertible [CON together + VERT to turn]—an automobile with a top that can be folded (turned) back

conversation [CON together + VERS to turn]—*lit.* a turning together for talk

controversy [CONTRA against + VERS to turn]—*lit.* opinions turned against each other; a dispute

avert (uh vurt') [AB away + VERT to turn]—to turn away. *She averted her eyes from the unpleasant scene.* Also, to prevent. *By taking preventive measures, they hope to avert another disaster.*

averse (uh vurs') [AB from + VERS to turn]—*lit.* to turn from; having a feeling of great distaste. *Having lost so much money on the lottery, she was averse to trying again.*

aversion (uh vur' zhun) [AB away + VERS to turn]—*lit.* a turning away; extreme dislike. *Because of her aversion to work, she never held a job long.*

adverse (ad vurs') [AD against + VERS to turn]—turned against; unfavorable. *The company had to cope with adverse publicity.*

adversary (ad' vur ser ē) [AD against + VERS to turn]—*lit.* one turned against another; opponent. *She easily defeated her adversary in the contest.*

adversity (ad vur' suh tē) [AD against + VERS to turn]—the state of being turned against; misfortune. *His years of adversity made him sympathetic to others in trouble.*

vertebra (vur' tuh bruh)—a bone of the spinal column that turns. *A vertebra is one of 20 short, thick bones through which the spinal cord runs.*

vertigo (vur' ti gō)—dizziness and the feeling that one's environment is whirling (turning) about. *After his illness he sometimes had attacks of vertigo.*

versatile (vur' suh tul)—able to turn easily from one subject or occupation to another; competent in many fields. *An unusually versatile actor, he is able to play any role from hero to clown.*

introvert (in' truh vurt) [INTRO within + VERT to turn]—*lit.* one who turns within; one whose thoughts and interests are directed inward. *Introverts think mainly about themselves.*

perverse (pur vurs') [PER (intensive) + VERS to turn]—turned away from what is right or good; obstinately disobedient or difficult. *Always perverse, he opposed the wishes of the group.*

obverse (ob vurs') [OB toward + VERS to turn]—turned toward the observer; the side bearing the main design (as opposed to reverse). *The obverse side of a U.S. coin bears the main design and the date.*

inadvertent (in ud vur' tunt) [IN not + AD to + VERT to turn]—*lit.* not turning one's mind to a matter; unintentional. *He made an inadvertent reference to the plans for the surprise party.*

ALSO: anniversary, averse, converse, conversion, diverse, diversify, diversion, divorce, extrovert, incontrovertible, inverse, invertebrate, revert, subversive, versus (vs.)

EXERCISE 1 Write the appropriate VERT, VERS word.

1. I'd rather have him as a partner than as an _____ in the game.
2. Instead of saying, "Heads or tails?" he always said, "_____ or reverse?"
3. I didn't mean to offend her, but she took offense at my _____ remark.
4. Spending much time analyzing his thoughts, he was a true _____.
5. Completely disillusioned, he was _____ to giving any money to the project.
6. No matter what I want, he is always _____ and wants the opposite.
7. During that year of _____, he lost his job and his home.

8. Our trip had to be postponed because of _____ weather.

9. When I glanced at her, she _____ her eyes.

10. My sister is a _____ person, equally good at tennis, oil painting, and cooking.

11. An _____ to a particular food can sometimes be traced to an allergy.

12. After her attack of _____, she feared walking up or down stairs without a handrail.

EXERCISE 2   REVIEW   Give the meaning of each root and a word in which it is found.

	MEANING	WORD
1. PHON		
2. POST		
3. PRE		
4. PRO		
5. RE		
6. SCRIB, SCRIPT		
7. SED, SID		
8. SPEC, SPIC, SPECT		
9. SUB		
10. SUPER		
11. SYN, SYM, SYL		
12. TELE		
13. TORT		
14. TRI		
15. VER		
16. VERT, VERS		

EXERCISE 3 REVIEW The ten underlined words are ones you've studied. Copy them below and fill in the blanks. For four words, you know two roots; for the rest, you've learned only one. Understanding all the words should make rereading the paragraph satisfying.

Faced with the prospect of chronic oil shortages, most Americans concur with the idea that everyone must conserve. Government edicts have reduced speed limits and controlled temperatures in public buildings. Many individuals have overcome their propensity to drive their cars to work and no longer regard public transportation with aversion. Others are experimenting with a spectrum of solutions from windmills to solar power. All of these efforts taken together, though not a panacea for our energy problems, are an important prologue to what we must accomplish in the future to make sure some oil supplies will be left for posterity.

	WORD	ROOT	ROOT MEANING	WORD MEANING
1.	_____	_____	_____	
		_____	_____	_____
2.	_____	_____	_____	_____
3.	_____	_____	_____	
		_____	_____	_____
4.	_____	_____	_____	
		_____	_____	_____
5.	_____	_____	_____	_____
6.	_____	_____	_____	_____
7.	_____	_____	_____	_____
8.	_____	_____	_____	_____
9.	_____	_____	_____	
		_____	_____	_____
10.	_____	_____	_____	_____

VIA—way

In Roman times a place where three roads met was called the three-*way* place or trivia (TRI three + VIA way), and when women on their way to market gathered at that place to chat about common, unimportant matters, their talk came to be called **trivia** or three-*way* talk. Eventually any talk about unimportant things was called **trivial**. So today, when we talk about trivial things, we are reminded of those Romans who did likewise.

via—by way of

viaduct [VIA way + DUC to lead]—a bridge leading a road (way) over a valley

previous [PRE before + VIA way]—under way beforehand

obvious [OB against + VIA way]—*lit.* standing against one in the way; clearly visible; evident

trivia (triv′ ē uh) [TRI three + VIA way]—*lit.* three-way talk; originally, the commonplace matters discussed when people met at the crossroads; any unimportant matters. *A knowledge of trivia is important for quiz show contestants.*

trivial (triv′ ē ul) [TRI three + VIA way]—unimportant. *She became upset over the most trivial things.*

deviate (dē′ vē āt) [DE from + VIA way]—to turn away from an established way. *Anyone who deviates from the rules is likely to be in trouble.*

deviation (dē vē ā′ shun) [DE from + VIA way]—a turning aside from an established way. *The chairperson would not tolerate the slightest deviation from parliamentary rules.*

devious (dē′ vē us) [DE from + VIA way]—straying from the proper way; crooked. *His fortune had been made by devious means.*

impervious (im pur′ vē us) [IN not + PER through + VIA way]—*lit.* no way through; incapable of being passed through. *The cloth was impervious to water. His mind was impervious to reason.*

obviate (ob′ vē āt) [OB against + VIA way]—*lit.* to come against something in the way and dispose of it; to prevent. *Careful planning will obviate future difficulties.*

EXERCISE 1   REVIEW   Write C in front of each sentence in which all words are used correctly.

_____   1. A rabbit chasing a dog would be preposterous.

_____   2. I have a predilection for anything red and always try to avoid that color.

_____ 3. Morpheus was so called because he was the god of the forms that sleepers see in their dreams.

_____ 4. The witness averred that she had never been in the building before.

_____ 5. The orchestra was practicing a polyphonic tone poem, with a single melody throughout.

_____ 6. Because she suffers from claustrophobia, she refused to go near the edge of the observation platform at the top of the building.

_____ 7. I wasn't thinking what I was saying when I made that inadvertent remark.

_____ 8. His former devious methods indicate that he never would participate in any questionable deals.

_____ 9. Having been a poor baseball player himself, he felt empathy with his son, who was having no luck in catching the ball.

_____ 10. The administration was apathetic and really working hard to further the new plan.

_____ 11. A pedigree means literally the foot of a crane because the three-line diagram used to indicate descent looks like the foot of a crane.

_____ 12. To most people it's cacophony, but I really enjoy the sounds of an orchestra tuning up.

_____ 13. She had learned to reason according to the old classic syllogisms.

_____ 14. If you follow the rules, you'll obviate further trouble.

_____ 15. Her perverse attitude made her a favorite in the office.

_____ 16. A book published posthumously is published after the author's death.

_____ 17. As they chatted about trivia during the musical, they were impervious to the glances of those around them.

_____ 18. As soon as the winner was announced, there was pandemonium in the stands.

_____ 19. The slightest deviation in following the recipe may mean failure.

_____ 20. A subservient employee is always afraid to deviate from the norm.

_____ 21. Walking home from the subway, we were caught in a veritable downpour.

_____ 22. You may depend upon her to give a veracious account of the proceedings.

_____ 23. The coin collector turned the coin over to look at the obverse side.

_____ 24. The officer at the border asked for veracity of my citizenship.

_____ 25. A true introvert, he went out of his way to make friends.

_____ 26. Always a versatile person, she could fit into any of several jobs.

VOC, VOKE—to call, voice

A **convocation** [CON together + VOC to call] is a *calling* together, an assembly. It may begin with an **invocation** [IN in + VOC to call], a *calling* for divine aid; and if the convocation is a college graduation, then the graduates will be looking forward to their **vocations** or *callings*. Later, after they are settled in their jobs, they will no doubt be thinking of **avocations** or *callings* away from their jobs.

vocal—produced by the voice; quick to speak or criticize

vocabulary—*lit.* the words one can speak (call)

vocation—a calling; an occupation or profession

avocation [AB away + VOC to call]—*lit.* a calling away; a diversion; a hobby

convocation [CON together + VOC to call]—*lit.* a calling together; an assembly

provoke [PRO forth + VOC to call]—to call forth; to bring about; to cause anger or irritation

provocation [PRO forth + VOC to call]—something that calls forth irritation

advocate [AD to + VOC to call]—*lit.* one called to give evidence; a person who pleads in another's behalf; a person who argues for a cause

revoke (ri vōk') [RE back + VOC to call]—to call back. *The company revoked its earlier offer.*

irrevocable (i rev' uh ku bul) [IN not + RE back + VOC to call]—not capable of being called back; unalterable. *His decision was irrevocable.*

invoke (in vōk') [IN in + VOC to call]—*lit.* to call in; to call upon for aid or support. *The accused person invoked the Fifth Amendment.*

invocation (in vuh kā' shun) [IN in + VOC to call]—*lit.* a calling for divine aid; an opening prayer. *The invocation was given by the dean.*

evoke (i vōk') [E out + VOC to call]—*lit.* to call out; to call forth, as memories or feelings. *The smell of burning leaves always evoked memories of his childhood.*

evocative (i vok' uh tiv) [E out + VOC to call]—*lit.* calling out; calling forth. *The sounds of the forest were evocative of his early camping days.*

vociferous (vō sif' ur us) [VOC voice + FER to carry]—*lit.* carrying a loud voice; noisy. *The crowd at the rally made a vociferous protest against the location of the nuclear power plant.*

ALSO: advocacy, equivocal, equivocate, provocative

EXERCISE 1   Write the appropriate VOC, VOKE word.

1. The final decision of the court was _____.

2. Looking at old photographs would always _____ memories of happy times.

3. The Pilgrims _____ God's help on their journey.

4. Although he liked his vocation, it was his _____ that
   really interested him.

5. When the holiday was canceled, there were _____
   complaints.

6. Going back to the town where he grew up was always an _____
   experience.

7. The graduation ceremony began with an _____.

8. Awards were presented at the spring _____.

9. Because of the accident, his driver's license was _____.

10. She was preparing not merely for a job but for a _____.

EXERCISE 2   REVIEW   Write C in front of each sentence in which all words
are used correctly.

_____ 1. I'm not averse to helping you with your plan.

_____ 2. She knew many recondite facts about gorillas.

_____ 3. The two countries made a trilateral agreement about arms limi-
           tation.

_____ 4. We were fascinated as we watched the metamorphosis of the pupa
           into a moth.

_____ 5. In the botany lab we dissected a flower and named all its parts.

_____ 6. We felt that the assessor gave too low an evaluation of our house.

_____ 7. Adverse road conditions made our trip pleasant.

_____ 8. The superpower tried to subjugate the natives on the island.

_____ 9. My adversary proved to be redoubtable.

_____ 10. The benevolence of the lodge members aided him in his time of
           adversity.

_____ 11. We were surprised at the remission of her illness.

EXERCISE 3   Make your final journal entry a slightly longer one, and make
use of as many of your new words as you can.

COMPREHENSIVE TEST A The words in this test contain the same roots as the words in the PRELIMINARY TEST on page 9. A comparison of your two scores will indicate how much the study of word roots has improved your vocabulary.

_____ 1. ambivalence   A.lack of feeling   B.conflicting feelings   C.jealousy   D.dislike

_____ 2. misanthropic   A.doubting   B.hating marriage   C.hating people   D.generous

_____ 3. antithesis   A.secondary theme of an essay   B.failure   C.climax   D.exact opposite

_____ 4. automaton   A.self-government   B.government by a single person   C.one who acts mechanically   D.car buff

_____ 5. beneficiary   A.lawyer who handles wills   B.one who receives benefits   C.one who gives money to benefit others   D.one who leaves money in a will

_____ 6. synchronize   A.to keep a time record   B.to compose an accompaniment   C.to cause to keep time together   D.to prophesy

_____ 7. circumspect   A.cautious   B.hardworking   C.knowledgeable   D.showing respect

_____ 8. compunction   A.connecting word   B.compulsion   C.satisfaction about something one has done   D.a slight regret

_____ 9. incredulous   A.not believing readily   B.believing too readily   C.lacking credit   D.not trustworthy

_____ 10. cursory   A.using profanity   B.critical   C.hateful   D.hasty and superficial

_____ 11. demagogue   A.ancient tribal god   B.half man and half god   C.leader who appeals to the emotions to gain power   D.leader who works for the good of the people

_____ 12. euphonious   A.having a pleasant sound   B.coming from a distance   C.false   D.difficult to hear

_____ 13. exonerate   A.to honor   B.to take out objectionable parts   C.to free from blame   D.to find guilty

_____ 14. eulogy   A.speech by an actor alone on the stage   B.explanation of a literary passage   C.speech blaming someone   D.speech praising someone

_____ 15. colloquial   A.incorrect   B.talkative   C.conversational   D.standard

_____ 16. malevolent   A.kindly   B.violent   C.giving money to others   D.wishing evil to others

_____ 17. emissary   A.traveler   B.spy   C.servant   D.someone sent out

_____ 18. anthropomorphic   A.relating to the early Stone Age   B.having human characteristics   C.having animal form   D.changing form

_____ 19. panoply   A.impressive display   B.high covering   C.harsh criticism D.series of games

_____ 20. apathetic   A.sad   B.deserving sympathy   C.pitiful   D.indifferent

_____ 21. expedite   A.to experiment with   B.to send away   C.to speed the progress of   D.to make clear

_____ 22. propensity   A.dislike   B.thoughtfulness   C.belief   D.natural inclination

_____ 23. sedentary   A.temporary   B.permanent   C.requiring much sitting D.producing sediment

_____ 24. specious   A.having many rooms   B.seemingly good but actually not so   C.reasonable   D.a category of living things

_____ 25. subterfuge   A.deceptive strategy   B.underwater vessel   C.play acting   D.hatred

_____ 26. insuperable   A.extraordinary   B.easily overcome   C.incapable of being overcome   D.best of its kind

_____ 27. symbiosis   A.similarity in biologic function   B.similarity in evolutionary development   C.living together in close relationship D. use of symbols in literature

COMPREHENSIVE TEST B These words contain all the roots you have studied. Give the meaning of each root and the meaning of the word.

		MEANING OF ROOT	MEANING OF WORD
1. amphibian	AMPHI	_____	
	BIO	_____	_____
2. antedate	ANTE	_____	_____
3. anthropomorphic	ANTHROP	_____	
	MORPH	_____	_____
4. antibiotic	ANTI	_____	
	BIO	_____	_____
5. asymmetric	A	_____	
	SYM	_____	
	METR	_____	_____
6. autograph	AUTO	_____	
	GRAPH	_____	_____
7. benediction	BENE	_____	
	DICT	_____	_____
8. biennial	BI	_____	
	ENN	_____	_____
9. chronometer	CHRON	_____	
	METER	_____	_____
10. circumscribe	CIRCUM	_____	
	SCRIB	_____	_____
11. colloquial	COL	_____	
	LOQU	_____	_____
12. convert	CON	_____	
	VERT	_____	_____
13. credible	CRED	_____	_____

		MEANING OF ROOT	MEANING OF WORD
14. discursive	DIS	_____	
	CUR	_____	_____
15. emissary	E	_____	
	MISS	_____	_____
16. equate	EQU	_____	
17. euphony	EU	_____	
	PHON	_____	_____
18. evoke	E	_____	
	VOC	_____	_____
19. expedient	EX	_____	
	PED	_____	_____
20. fidelity	FID	_____	_____
21. genealogy	GEN	_____	
	-LOGY	_____	_____
22. malady	MAL	_____	_____
23. monogram	MONO	_____	
	GRAM	_____	_____
24. pandemic	PAN	_____	
	DEM	_____	_____
25. philanthropy	PHIL	_____	
	ANTHROP	_____	_____
26. phobia	PHOBIA	_____	_____
27. preposterous	PRE	_____	
	POST	_____	_____
28. prologue	PRO	_____	
	LOG	_____	_____
29. prospectus	PRO	_____	
	SPECT	_____	_____

		MEANING OF ROOT	MEANING OF WORD
30. retort	RE	_____	
	TORT	_____	_____
31. subside	SUB	_____	
	SID	_____	_____
32. superannuated	SUPER	_____	
	ANN	_____	_____
33. telepathy	TELE	_____	
	PATH	_____	_____
34. trivia	TRI	_____	
	VIA	_____	_____
35. verify	VER	_____	_____

COMPREHENSIVE TEST C   The words in these sentences contain all the roots you have studied. Put a C in front of each sentence in which all words are used correctly.

_____ 1. He felt apathetic about his job, not caring whether he kept it or not.

_____ 2. The bald eagle, an amphibian, is the national bird of the United States.

_____ 3. A triennial convention is held every three years.

_____ 4. My mother plants perennials so she won't have to buy new plants each year.

_____ 5. The anterior legs of an animal are those at the front.

_____ 6. Gorillas and zebras are anthropoids.

_____ 7. Our contestant found that he faced a powerful antagonist.

_____ 8. Taking no interest in her work, she performed it like an automaton.

_____ 9. That insurance salesperson has a benign attitude toward clients, trying to help them make the best choices.

_____ 10. A diameter bisects a circle.

_____ 11. A biopsy is an examination of tissues from a living body.

_____ 12. A chronic disease lasts a long time.

_____ 13. She takes forever to say anything because she uses so many circumlocutions.

_____ 14. A coherent paper is well organized and sticks to the point.

_____ 15. A four-year-old is amazingly credulous and will believe anything you say.

_____ 16. Television was the precursor of radio.

_____ 17. An endemic plant is one that is widespread over the entire earth.

_____ 18. A jurisdiction is a sentence given by a judge to someone who is guilty.

_____ 19. I was disconcerted by their failure to come on time.

_____ 20. Becoming upset over the criticism, he lost his usual equanimity.

_____ 21. After I lost that tennis match, I was in a state of euphoria.

_____ 22. Receiving that scholarship expedited my getting through college.

_____ 23. She accused him of fidelity and threatened to get a divorce.

_____ 24. He has always been diffident and dreads speaking in public.

_____ 25. Praise often engenders greater loyalty in employees.

_____ 26. By using many details, he gave a graphic picture of the storm.

_____ 27. The first scene of the play was a monologue between two characters.

_____ 28. Studying word roots in this book has given me an interest in etymology.

_____ 29. That day she was unusually loquacious, spending hours talking to me.

_____ 30. I missed class because I was really ill; I wasn't malingering.

_____ 31. The odometer indicated that my blood pressure was above normal.

_____ 32. A missive is a weapon.

_____ 33. Monogamy is the belief that there is only one God.

_____ 34. The lecturer's presentation was simply an amorphous collection of unrelated stories.

_____ 35. Do you expect the encounter group to be a panacea for all your problems?

_____ 36. She felt extreme antipathy for her sister and liked to spend as much time with her as she could.

_____ 37. Improving my vocabulary has impeded my ability to read with understanding.

_____ 38. He's a born philanthropist, criticizing everyone and in general hating people.

_____ 39. Because she suffers from claustrophobia, she dislikes riding in elevators.

_____ 40. Polyphonic means having two or more melodies combined.

_____ 41. Because I want to leave a record for posterity, I'm writing our family history.

_____ 42. Being given a month's vacation was unprecedented; no one had ever been given that long a vacation before.

_____ 43. As a proponent of conservation, he has been making speeches advocating paper recycling.

_____ 44. Now that she has established new habits, she's not likely to revert to the old ones.

_____ 45. A new employee needs to be circumspect about asking for favors.

_____ 46. Abe Lincoln ascribed his success to his mother.

_____ 47. If I take a sedentary job, I won't get enough exercise.

_____ 48. When I was in France, I didn't find my inability to speak French an insuperable barrier.

_____ 49. Symbiosis is the living together of two different organisms in what is usually a mutually beneficial relationship.

_____ 50. Telepathy is the sending of messages by Morse code.

_____ 51. The tortuous mountain road was nothing but twists and turns.

_____ 52. He went sailing on the lake in his subterfuge.

_____ 53. I had no reason to doubt his veracity because he had never lied to me.

_____ 54. There were vociferous complaints about the new zoning laws.

CHALLENGE TEST   Here is a test on words you haven't studied. They are from the 164 roots in the second part of the text. Test yourself, and then look up any words you miss in the Word Index (p. 193) to find the page where the word is defined.

_____ 1. impunity   A.weakness   B.punishment   C.freedom from punishment

_____ 2. carnivorous   A.plant-eating   B.flesh-eating   C.eating everything

_____ 3. mortify   A.to join or fasten securely   B.to humiliate   C.to provoke

_____ 4. heterogeneous   A.composed of similar kinds   B.composed of different kinds   C.not conforming to accepted opinions

_____ 5. complacent   A.self-satisfied   B.placed correctly   C.placed together

_____ 6. acrimonious   A.sharp or bitter in speech   B.stingy   C.able to get along well with others

_____ 7. presentiment   A.foreknowledge   B.sentimental gift C.an audience with an important person

_____ 8. tenet   A.something one isn't sure of   B.belief one holds   C.renter

_____ 9. culpable   A.successful   B.informed   C.blameworthy

_____ 10. sinecure   A.cure for sinus problems   B.something without a cure   C.a soft job

_____ 11. abridge   A.to put a bridge across   B.to remove a bridge   C.to condense

_____ 12. approbation   A.official approval   B.probation   C.freedom from probation

_____ 13. archetype   A.original model   B.type of Roman temple   C.architectural drawing

_____ 14. absolve   A.to resolve a conflict   B.to treat a wound   C.to free from blame or guilt

_____ 15. elucidate   A.to date a manuscript   B.to make clear by explanation   C.to remove from consideration

_____ 16. verbiage   A.small leaves   B.forest growth   C.wordiness

_____ 17. prognosticate   A.to predict   B.to chew thoroughly   C.to swear

_____ 18. exhume   A.to smoke   B.to bury   C.to remove from a grave

_____ 19. obsequious   A.overly submissive   B.overly proud   C.overly bossy

_____ 20. conifer   A.to cheat   B.to discuss with   C.a cone-bearing tree

_____ 21. pervade   A.to persuade   B.to march   C.to spread throughout

_____ 22. omniscient   A.all-powerful   B.all-knowing   C.present everywhere

_____ 23. hyperbole   A.mathematical figure   B.spacecraft   C.overstatement

_____ 24. conducive   A.tending to hinder   B.tending to aid   C.helping to reduce

164 ADDITIONAL ROOTS

Browsing through the following list will not only add some new words to your vocabulary but will also add more meaning to words you already know. The first definition is often a literal one (marked *lit.*) taken directly from the roots; the definitions that follow are the current ones.

Many of the extra words, which are listed but not defined, are defined elsewhere in the book. To find any particular word, check the Word Index on page 193.

AB   away, from, off

abduct [AB away + DUC to lead]—*lit.* to lead away by force; to kidnap

abscond [AB away + COND to hide]—to run away and hide, especially to escape the law

abominate [AB away + OMEN a bad omen]—*lit.* to turn away from a bad omen; to loathe, as to abominate cheaters

abstruse [AB away + TRUS to push]—*lit.* pushed away or hidden; hard to understand, as an abstruse theory

ALSO: abdicate, aberration, abject, abjure, abrogate, abrupt, absolve, abstemious, avert, avocation

AC, ACR   sharp

acute—sharp; severe, as an acute illness

acumen—sharpness of mind; sharp insight, as great business acumen

acrimonious—sharp or bitter in speech, as an acrimonious reply

exacerbate—to make sharper; to increase the severity of, as worry may exacerbate an illness

ALSO: acerbic, acerbity, acid, acrid, acrimony, acuity

ACRO   topmost, high

acropolis [ACRO high + POLI city]—the fortified height of an ancient Greek city, as the Acropolis in Athens

acrobat [ACRO high + BAT to walk]—*lit.* walking on tiptoes; a tumbler or performer on the tightrope; a performer of gymnastic feats

acronym [ACRO topmost + ONYM name]—a name made up from the initial (topmost) letters of several words, as NATO for North Atlantic Treaty Organization

acrostic—a verse in which the first (topmost) letters of the lines, when read vertically, form a word, as   **N**orth
  East
  West
  South

ALSO: acrophobia

143

AD   to, toward, against

adhere [AD to + HER to stick]—to stick fast to; to stay firm in supporting, as to adhere to a plan

adjudicate [AD to + JUD judge]—to hear and decide (a case); to act as judge, as to adjudicate a music contest

abet [AD to + BET to bait (a bear)]—to encourage, especially in wrongdoing, as to abet a thief

accumulate [AD to + CUMUL heap or pile up]—to heap or pile up, as to accumulate a fortune

ALSO: acclamation, addict, adjunct, advent, adversary, adversity, advertise, advocate, affluent, ascribe

AGR   field

agriculture [AGR field + CULT cultivation]—*lit.* cultivation of fields

agronomy—the science of raising field crops

agrarian—relating to the ownership of land, as agrarian disputes

peregrination [PER through + AGR field]—*lit.* travel through fields; travel from place to place

ALB   white

albino—an organism lacking normal skin, hair, and eye color, as an albino animal with white hair or fur and red eyes

albumen—a nutritive protein surrounding a developing embryo, as the white of an egg

album—a book with white (blank) pages

Albion—poetic name for England (after the white cliffs of Dover)

ALG   pain

neuralgia [NEUR nerve + ALG pain]—pain along a nerve

nostalgia [NOSTOS return home + ALG pain]—desire to return in thought or in fact to a former time in one's life, as nostalgia for one's childhood home

analgesic [AN without + ALG pain]—a medication that reduces pain

ALTER   other

alter ego [ALTER other + EGO self]—another side of oneself

altercation—a heated argument with another

subaltern [SUB below + ALTER other]—*lit.* below another; a subordinate

altruism—concern for the welfare of others

ALSO: alter, alteration, alternate, alternative, alternator, altruist

AM   to love

amiable—good-natured and friendly

amicable—showing friendliness and good will, as amicable relations between nations

amity—peaceful relations, as amity between nations

amateur—one who engages in some art, science, or sport for the love of it rather than for money

ALSO: amatory, amorous, amours, Amy, paramour

ANIM mind, soul, spirit, passion

animate—to give life or spirit to

unanimity [UNI one + ANIM mind]—*lit.* of one mind; complete agreement, as the unanimity of a committee

animus—an animating motive or intention; a feeling of strong hatred, as a feeling of animus toward one's boss

animosity—bitter hostility or open enmity

ALSO: animadversion, animal, animated, animation, equanimity, inanimate, magnanimous, pusillanimous, unanimous

AQUA water

aquatic—living in or near water, as aquatic plants; taking place in or on water, as aquatic sports

aquacade—an exhibition of swimming and diving

aquamarine [AQUA water + MAR sea]—the bluish green color of seawater

aqueduct [AQUA water + DUC to lead]—a pipe or channel for transporting (leading) water from a distance

ALSO: Aqua-lung, aquaplane, aquarium, Aquarius, aqueous, aquaculture

ARCH (1) chief, ruler (first in power)

archbishop—chief bishop

archenemy—chief enemy

architect [ARCH chief + TECT builder]—chief builder

patriarch [PATER father + ARCH ruler]—the father and ruler of a family or tribe

ALSO: anarchy, archangel, matriarch, monarchy, oligarchy

ARCH (2) ancient, first (first in time)

archives—an organized body of records of an organization (from the beginning)

archetype—an original (first) type or model after which other similar things are patterned

archaic—belonging to an ancient period, as the archaic word *methinks*

archaism—an archaic word or expression

ALSO: archeology

ASTER, ASTR star

astronomy [ASTR star + NOM law]—the science of the laws of the stars

astronaut [ASTR star + NAUT sailor]—*lit.* a sailor among the stars; a space traveler

sterling—silver of the highest quality, so called from the star originally stamped on it

asterisk—a star-shaped figure (*) referring to a footnote

ALSO: aster, asteroid, astrology, astronomical, disaster

AUD to hear

audible—loud enough to be heard

audition—a trial test or hearing

audience—those assembled to hear or see

auditorium—a room for hearing a performance

ALSO: audiovisual, audit, auditor, inaudible

AVI   bird

aviary—a large cage for keeping birds
avian—pertaining to or characteristic of birds
aviator—the pilot of an airplane; flier
aviation—the science of flying airplanes
ALSO: auspicious

BELL   war

rebellion [RE again + BELL war]—*lit.* waging war again;
   a resistance to authority
rebel [RE again + BELL war]—one who resists authority
belligerent—warlike; hostile, as belligerent nations
bellicose—hostile in manner or temperament; eager to
   quarrel or fight, as a bellicose disposition
ALSO: antebellum

BIBL   book

Bible—originally, The Book
bibliography [BIBL book + GRAPH to write]—a (written) list of books on a specific subject
bibliomania [BIBL book + MANIA craze]—a craze for
   collecting books
ALSO: bibliophile

BREV   short

brevity—shortness of duration; conciseness
abbreviation [AD to + BREV short]—shortened form of
   a word or phrase
brief—short in length or extent
abridge [AD to + BREV short]—*lit.* to make short; to
   condense, as to abridge a report

CAD, CID, CAS
to fall

cadence—a falling inflection of the voice; rhythmical
   movement of language; in music, a progression of chords
   moving to a harmonious close
cascade—a waterfall over steep rocks
coincidental [CO together + in on + CID to fall]—*lit.*
   falling on together; happening together
Occident—*lit.* the lands of the setting (falling) sun; the
   lands west of Asia, especially Europe and the Western
   Hemisphere
ALSO: accident, casualty, casuistry, decadence, deciduous, incident

CAND   white,
   glowing

candle—a cylindrical mass of (originally white) tallow or
   wax containing a wick burned to give light
incandescent [IN (an intensive) + CAND glowing]—
   glowing with light as a result of being heated, as an
   incandescent light bulb
candid—*lit.* white, pure; free from prejudice; frank, as a
   candid reply
candidate—one seeking an office, so called because of the
   white toga worn by candidates for office in ancient
   Rome
ALSO: candor

CAP to take

caption—a heading that takes one's attention, as the caption accompanying a photograph

captious—designed to take in or entrap, as captious questions; fond of catching others in mistakes and of finding fault with trivial details, as a captious disposition

capacious—able to take or contain a large quantity; spacious, as a capacious attic

capacitor—a device consisting of two or more conducting plates separated by an insulating material and used for storing an electric charge

ALSO: capable, capacity, captivate, captive, capture, incapacitate

CAPIT head

capital—head city; head letter in a word; main (head) wealth

decapitate [DE away + CAPIT head]—to cut the head away from the body

capitulate—*lit.* to draw up the head or chief items for surrender; to surrender on prearranged conditions

recapitulate [RE again + CAPIT head]—to summarize again the head or chief items

ALSO: biceps, capitalism, captain, per capita, precipitate

CARN flesh, meat

carnivorous [CARN flesh + VOR to eat]—flesh-eating (as opposed to herbivorous, plant-eating)

incarnate [IN in + CARN flesh]—embodied in human form, as God incarnate in Jesus

carnal—relating to the desires and appetites of the flesh; sensual, as carnal sins

carnival [CARN meat + LEVARE to take away]—*lit.* meat taken away; a time of merrymaking and feasting, especially the time just before Lent, when meat was taken away

ALSO: carnation, chile con carne, reincarnation

CATA down

catastrophe [CATA down + STROPH to turn]—*lit.* an overturning; a great and sudden disaster

cataract—a great downpour; a large waterfall

cataclysm [CATA down + KLUZEIN to wash]—a devastating flood; a violent upheaval or disaster

catapult [CATA down + PALLEIN to hurl]—a mechanism for launching an airplane without a runway, as from the deck of a ship

CED, CEED, CESS
to go, to yield

cede—to yield or surrender possession of, as to cede a property to someone

precede [PRE before + CED to go]—to go before

intercede [INTER between + CED to go]—*lit.* to go between; to plead in behalf of another

concede [CON with + CED to go]—*lit.* to go along with; to yield, as to concede victory to the other team

ALSO: accede, ancestor, antecedent, precedent, predecessor, proceed, recede, recession, secede, unprecedented

CENT hundred

cent—1/100 of a dollar

century—100 years

centigrade—a temperature scale divided in 100 degrees; Celsius

centimeter [CENT hundred + METER measure]—a unit of length equal to 1/100 of a meter

ALSO: bicentennial, centenarian, centennial, centipede, centurion, percent

CHROM color

monochromatic [MONO one + CHROM color]—having only one color

polychromatic [POLY many + CHROM color]—having many colors

chromosome [CHROM color + SOM body]—a DNA-containing, rod-shaped body of the cell nuclei of plants and animals (so-called because it stains intensely with basic dyes)

chromatic scale—a musical scale consisting of 13 semitones (shades of tone)

ALSO: panchromatic

CID, CIS to cut,
to kill

suicide [SUI self + CID to kill]—the intentional killing of oneself

decide [DE off + CID to cut]—*lit.* to cut off hesitating; to make up one's mind

incisive [IN in + CIS to cut]—*lit.* cutting into; penetrating, as incisive remarks

insecticide—a substance used to kill insects

ALSO: concise, excise, genocide, germicide, herbicide, homicide, incision, incisor, precise, scissors

CIV citizen

civic—pertaining to a city or to citizens

civil—pertaining to citizens; proper; polite

civility—politeness; courtesy

uncivil [UN not + CIV citizen]—not civil; discourteous, as an uncivil tongue

ALSO: civilian, civilization, civilize

CLAM to cry out

clamor—a loud outcry or shouting; any loud and sustained noise

proclamation [PRO before + CLAM to cry out]—an official public announcement

acclamation [AD to + CLAM to cry out]—an oral vote, especially an enthusiastic vote of approval taken without formal ballot, as a motion passed by acclamation

reclaim [RE back + CLAM to cry out]—to call back; to bring back to a useful condition, as to reclaim aluminum from old cans

ALSO: acclaim, claim, declaim, declamatory, disclaim, exclaim, proclaim

CLAR clear

clarity—clearness

clarion—a medieval trumpet with a clear, shrill tone; clear and shrill, as a clarion call

clarinet—a woodwind instrument, probably named after the medieval clarion

clairvoyance [CLAR clear + VID to see]—the supposed power to see clearly things not in sight

ALSO: clarify, declare

CLUD, CLUS, CLAUS, CLOS to close, to shut

seclude [SE apart + CLUD to shut]—to shut apart from others; to place in solitude

exclude [EX out + CLUD to shut]—to shut out; to prevent from entering; to leave out

cloister—*lit.* a closed place; a place of religious seclusion, as a monastery or convent

closet—a small closed place for storing things

ALSO: clause, claustrophobia, close, conclude, disclose, enclose, include, preclude, recluse

CONTRA, COUNTER against

contraband [CONTRA against + BANNUS decree]—against the law, as contraband or smuggled goods

contraindicate—*lit.* to indicate against; to make inadvisable, as a certain medicine is contraindicated

contradistinction—distinction by contrast, as a job in contradistinction to a vocation

countermand [COUNTER against + MAND command]—*lit.* against a command; to cancel or reverse a command or order

ALSO: contradict, contrary, contretemps, controversy, counterfeit, counterpart, counterpoint, counterproductive, counterrevolutionary, countersign

CORD, CARD
heart

cardiac—pertaining to the heart
cordial—warm, hearty
concord [CON together + CORD heart]—*lit.* hearts together; agreement; friendly and peaceful relations
discord [DIS apart + CORD heart]—*lit.* hearts apart; lack of agreement
ALSO: accord, cardiogram, record

CORP body

corpse—dead body
corporation—a body of persons legally allowed to act as one person (body)
corps—a body of troops
corpulent—having a fat body
ALSO: corporal, corporate, corpus, corpuscle, corsage, corset, incorporate

COSM universe,
order

cosmic—relating to the universe
cosmopolitan [COSM universe + POLI city]—*lit.* like a citizen of the universe; at home in all parts of the world; common to the whole world
cosmonaut [COSM universe + NAUT sailor]—*lit.* a sailor in the universe; a space traveler
cosmetic—a preparation to bring beauty (order) to the complexion
ALSO: cosmos, microcosm

CRAT, CRAC
to rule

democrat [DEM people + CRAT to rule]—one who believes in government by elected representatives of the people
aristocrat [ARISTOS best + CRAT to rule]—one of the hereditary ruling class or nobility
bureaucrat—an official who insists on rigid adherence to rules, forms, and routines
plutocrat [PLUT wealth + CRAT to rule]—a member of the governing wealthy class; a person who gains power or influence through wealth
ALSO: autocracy, autocrat, democracy, democratize, technocracy

CRYPT hidden

crypt—an underground chamber, especially one beneath a church that is used as a burial place
cryptic—mystifying; having a secret meaning, as a cryptic message
cryptography [CRYPT hidden + GRAPH to write]—the art of writing in or deciphering code
encryption—a process for scrambling access codes to computer programs to prevent illicit entry and control of the system
ALSO: Apocrypha, cryptogram, cryptogenic, cryptographer, decryption

CULP blame

culprit—a person blamed for a crime or an offense

culpable—deserving blame, as a culpable employee

exculpate [EX out + CULP blame]—*lit.* to take the blame out; to free from blame

mea culpa [(Latin) through my fault]—*lit.* I am to blame; an acknowledgment of a personal error or fault

CUR care

curator—one who takes care of a museum

secure [SE without + CUR care]—*lit.* without care; safe

sinecure [SINE without + CUR care]—*lit.* a position without care; a position not requiring much work

manicure [MANU hand + CUR care]—care of the hands or nails

ALSO: accurate, curate, curative, cure, curious, incurable, insecure, pedicure, procure, security

CYCL circle

cyclone—a windstorm whirling in a circle

bicycle [BI two + CYCL circle]—*lit.* two circles; a two-wheeled vehicle

encyclopedia [EN in + CYCL circle + PAIDEIA education]—*lit.* well-rounded education; a reference work on a wide range of subjects

cyclic or cyclical—recurring in cycles; a business or stock whose earnings fluctuate widely according to the economy

ALSO: cycle, Cyclops, cyclotron, encyclical, motorcycle, tricycle, unicycle

DE away, down, off, from, apart, completely

demote [DE down + MOT to move]—to move down to a lower rank, as to demote a soldier from corporal to private

derelict [DE completely + RE behind + LICT to leave] —*lit.* completely left behind; a homeless, jobless person; a vagrant

deciduous [DE off + CAD to fall]—*lit.* falling off; shedding leaves, as a deciduous tree

détente [DE apart + TEND to stretch]—a relaxing or easing of tension, as détente between nations

ALSO: decapitate, deflect, dehydrate, dejected, demise, deportment, desolate, deter, deviate, devolve

DEC ten

decathlon [DEC ten + ATHLON contest]—an athletic contest in which each contestant takes part in ten different track and field events

decimate—originally, to select by lot and kill every tenth one of; now, to destroy a large part, as famine may decimate a population

December—*lit.* the tenth month, so called in the ancient Roman calendar, which began with March

Decalogue [DEC ten + LOG word]—the Ten Commandments

ALSO: decade, decibel, decimal, decimeter

DENT tooth

dentist—one who cares for the teeth

dentifrice [DENT tooth + FRIC to rub]—a substance for cleaning the teeth

indent [IN in + DENT tooth]—to put a toothlike space in from the margin, as to indent a paragraph

dandelion—a plant so named because its deeply indented leaves resemble the *dent de lion* (French for "tooth of a lion")

ALSO: dentine, denture, trident

DERM skin

dermatology [DERM skin + -LOGY study of]—the study of skin diseases

dermatitis [DERM skin + -ITIS inflammation]—inflammation of the skin

taxidermy [TAX arrangement + DERM skin]—the stuffing and arranging of the skins of dead animals

pachyderm [PACHY thick + DERM skin]—any thick-skinned, hoofed mammal, especially an elephant

ALSO: epidermis, hypodermic

DIA through, between

diameter [DIA through + METER measure]—the measurement through the center of a circle

diathermy [DIA through + THERM heat]—a treatment that generates heat in body tissues by high-frequency electric current

diaphanous [DIA through + PHAN to show]—showing through; transparent, as a diaphanous veil

diatribe [DIA through + TRIB to rub]—*lit.* a rubbing through; a bitter and abusive criticism, as uttering a diatribe against one's supervisor

ALSO: diagnosis, diagonal, diagram, dialogue, diaphragm, diatonic

DOMIN master

dominate—to control by superior authority or power

domain—*lit.* a place where one is master; a range of rule or control

predominant [PRE before + DOMIN master]—*lit.* master before all others; having superior strength, influence, or authority; most common, as the predominant color in a design

indomitable [IN not + DOMIN master]—not capable of being mastered; unconquerable

ALSO: dominant, domineer, dominion, predominate

DUC, DUCT
to lead

induct [IN in + DUC to lead]—*lit.* to lead in; to bring into military service

conductor [CON together + DUC to lead]—one who leads people together, as a symphony conductor

conducive [CON together + DUC to lead]—leading to a result; tending to promote or assist, as quiet is conducive to study

deduce [DE down + DUC to lead]—*lit.* to lead down from; to conclude from known facts

ALSO: abduct, aqueduct, conduit, deductive, duct, ductile, duke, educate, introduce, viaduct

DUR   hard, lasting

durable—lasting; able to withstand wear

duress—hard treatment; force, as a confession signed under duress

dour—hard; gloomy, as a dour character

obdurate [OB against + DUR hard]—hardened against something; obstinate; stubborn

ALSO: duration, during, endure, enduring

DYN, DYNAM
power

dynamite—a powerful explosive

dynamic—forceful (powerful), as a dynamic leader

dynamo—a generator for producing heat (power); also, a forceful person

dynasty—a family that maintains power for several generations

ALSO: hydrodynamics, thermodynamics

EPI   on, upon

epidermis [EPI upon + DERM skin]—the outer (upon) layer of skin

epitaph [EPI upon + TAPH tomb]—an inscription on a tombstone

epithet [EPI upon + THET to place]—a descriptive term placed upon a person, as the epithet "gold digger"

epitome (i pit′ uh mē) [EPI upon + TOM to cut]—*lit.* to cut short; a summary; a representative of a class or type, as Solomon was the epitome of wisdom

ALSO: epicenter, epidemic, epigram, epilogue, episode, epitomize

ERG, URG   work

erg—a unit of work or energy in the metric system

energetic—showing capacity for work

energize—to give energy to; to enable to work

metallurgy—the science of working with metals; the art of separating metals from their ores

ALSO: energy, George, ergonomics, synergistic

ERR to wander

err—to wander from the truth or from accepted standards
error—something that wanders from what is correct or true
erratic—wandering; lacking regularity, as erratic behavior
aberration [AB from + ERR to wander]—a departure from what is right, true, correct; a departure from the normal or typical
ALSO: errant, errata, erroneous

EXTRA outside, beyond

extraterrestrial [EXTRA outside + TERR earth]—occurring outside the earth or its atmosphere
extramural [EXTRA outside + MUR wall]—occurring outside the walls or limits of a city or school, as extramural activities
extraneous—coming from the outside; not essential, as extraneous details in an essay
extrovert [EXTRA outside + VERT to turn]—one whose thoughts are turned outside; one interested in others or in the environment (in contrast to an introvert, whose thoughts are turned in)
ALSO: extracurricular, extralegal, extraordinary, extravagant, extravaganza

FAC, FIC
to make, to do

manufacture [MANU hand + FAC to make]—originally, to make by hand; now, to produce
facility—ease of doing, as a facility in spotting word roots
facilitate—to make easier, as a large vocabulary facilitates reading
efficacy—the ability to achieve results; effectiveness
ALSO: artificial, benefactor, benefit, discomfit, facsimile, factory, factotum, faculty, malefactor, proficient

FER to carry, to bear

ferry—a boat for carrying passengers
infer [IN in + FER to carry]—*lit.* to carry in extra meaning; to conclude from something known or assumed
conifer [CON cone + FER to bear]—a cone-bearing evergreen tree
pestiferous [PEST plague + FER to carry]—*lit.* plague-carrying; bothersome, as all the pestiferous little details
ALSO: Christopher, circumference, confer, fertile, prefer, refer, referee, suffer, transfer, vociferous

FIN end

fine—*lit.* the end; a final payment of money for an offense, as a fine for illegal parking
finale—the end part, as the finale of a musical composition
infinite [IN not + FIN end]—not having an end
definitive [DE down + FIN end]—providing a final solution; conclusive; authoritative and complete, as a definitive biography
ALSO: affinity, confine, define, final, finance, finish, finite, indefinite, infinity, refine

FLECT, FLEX to bend	flexible—capable of being bent reflect [RE back + FLECT to bend]—to bend back, as waves of light, heat, or sound; to bend back one's thoughts, as to reflect on the past deflect [DE away + FLECT to bend]—to bend away from a course; to turn aside, as the wind deflects a boat from its course genuflect [GENU knee + FLECT to bend]—to bend the knee; to kneel, as in worship ALSO: flex, inflect, inflection, inflexible
FLU to flow	fluent—flowing smoothly; able to write or speak easily and rapidly, as a fluent lecturer confluence [CON together + FLU to flow]—a flowing together of two or more streams affluent [AD to + FLU to flow]—flowing in abundance; wealthy, as affluent neighbors mellifluous [MELL honey + FLU to flow]—flowing with honey or sweetness, as a mellifluous voice ALSO: fluctuate, fluid, flume, fluvial, flux, influence, influenza, influx, superfluous
FORT strong	fortify—to strengthen comfort—to give strength and hope to fortitude—the strength to endure misfortune with courage forte (pronounced fort)—one's strong point, as tennis is her forte; forte (pronounced for′ tā)—in music, loud or strong ALSO: effort, fort, fortification, fortissimo, fortress
FRAG, FRACT to break	fragile—easily broken fraction—a part broken off infraction [IN in + FRACT to break]—a breaking of a law refractory [RE back + FRACT to break]—*lit.* breaking back; obstinate; hard to manage, as a refractory child ALSO: fractious, fracture, fragile, fragment, frail, infringe, refract
FRATER brother	fraternal—brotherly fraternity—a group of men associated for some common purpose fraternize—to associate in a brotherly way; to mix intimately with the people of an enemy group (said of soldiers occupying enemy territory) confraternity—a group of persons devoted to a religious or charitable cause ALSO: fratricide, friar

FUS   to pour

refuse [RE back + FUS to pour]—*lit.* to pour back; to decline to accept, give, or allow

diffuse [DIF apart + FUS to pour]—poured or spread apart; not concentrated; not concise, as diffuse writing

suffuse [SUB below + FUS to pour]—to spread through or over, as the sky was suffused with color

effusive [E out + FUS to pour]—*lit.* poured out; unrestrained; too demonstrative, as effusive praise

ALSO: confuse, infuse, profuse, profusion, transfusion

GAM   marriage

bigamist [BI two + GAM marriage]—someone who marries one person while still married to another

monogamist [MONO one + GAM marriage]—one who is married to only one person at a time

polygamist [POLY many + GAM marriage]—one who is married to two or more persons at a time

misogamist [MIS to hate + GAM marriage]—one who hates marriage

ALSO: bigamy, gamete, misogamy, monogamy, polygamy

GEO   earth

geocentric—having the earth as a center, as a belief in a geocentric universe

apogee [APO from + GEO earth]—the point in the orbit of the moon when it is farthest from the earth

perigee [PERI near + GEO earth]—the point in the orbit of the moon when it is nearest to the earth

geodesic dome—a domed structure of lightweight straight elements that form interlocking polygons; having a curve like the curvature of the earth

ALSO: geode, geography, geology, geometry, George

GNOS   to know

diagnosis [DIA through + GNOS to know]—*lit.* a knowing or seeing through; the identification of a disease; an analysis of something

prognosis [PRO before + GNOS to know]—*lit.* a knowing beforehand; a forecasting of the probable course of a disease

prognosticate [PRO before + GNOS to know]—to know beforehand; to predict

ALSO: agnostic, Gnosticism, physiognomy

GREG   flock, herd

congregation [CON together + GREG flock]—*lit.* a flocking together; a group of people gathered together for worship

segregate [SE apart + GREG flock]—*lit.* to set apart from the flock; to separate from others

gregarious—tending to flock together; sociable

egregious [E out + GREG herd]—*lit.* separated out of the herd because of undesirable qualities; outstandingly bad, as an egregious error

ALSO: aggregate, congregate

HELIO sun

heliocentric—having the sun as the center

helium—a gaseous element so named because it was first observed in the sun's atmosphere

heliotrope [HELIO sun + TROP to turn]—plants with clusters of small white or reddish-purple flowers that turn toward the sun

HETERO different

heterogeneous [HETERO different + GEN kind]—composed of different kinds (in contrast to homogeneous, composed of similar kinds)

heterosexual—pertaining to different sexes (in contrast to homosexual, pertaining to the same sex)

heterodox [HETERO different + DOX opinion]—*lit.* having different opinions; not conforming to accepted opinions or beliefs, especially in religion (in contrast to orthodox, pertaining to accepted opinions)

HOMO (1) human

homicide [HOMO human + CID to kill]—the killing of one person by another

homage—originally, the allegiance of a vassal (human) to a feudal lord; now, honor publicly expressed to a person or idea

Homo sapiens [HOMO human + SAPIENS wise]—the scientific name for human beings

HOMO (2) same

homogenize [HOMO same + GEN kind]—to make the same throughout, as to homogenize milk

homogeneous [HOMO same + GEN kind]—composed of similar parts or kinds, as a homogeneous group of people

homosexual—being attracted to those of the same sex as oneself

homologous [HOMO same + LOGOS proportion]—having the same relative position, structure, or function and corresponding in evolutionary origin, as the flippers of a seal and the arms of a human are homologous

ALSO: anomaly, homonym, homophone

HUM ground

humus—the organic part of the soil made from decaying leaves and other vegetable matter

exhume [EX out + HUM ground]—*lit.* to take out of the ground; to remove from a grave

humble—*lit.* close to the ground; low in rank or position; modest

humiliate—to humble; to lower the pride or dignity of

ALSO: humility

HYDR water

hydroplane—a motorboat that can skim the surface of the water at high speeds

hydraulic—operated by water or other fluid, as a hydraulic brake or press

dehydrate [DE from + HYDR water]—to remove water from

hydroelectric—producing electricity by waterpower

ALSO: hydrant, hydrodynamics, hydrogen, hydrophobia

HYPER over

hypersensitive—oversensitive

hyperactive—overactive; abnormally active, as a hyperactive child

hypertension—*lit.* over tension; excessive tension; high blood pressure

hyperbole [HYPER over + BOL to throw]—*lit.* a throwing over or beyond; an overstatement, as weeping gallons of tears is a hyperbole

ALSO: hypercritical

HYPO under

hypodermic [HYPO under + DERM skin]—injected under the skin

hypothesis [HYPO under + THES to place]—a theory placed under investigation

hypotenuse [HYPO under + TEND to stretch]—*lit.* a line stretched under the right angle; the side of a right triangle opposite the right angle

hypochondria [HYPO under + CHONDR cartilage]—*lit.* a feeling under the cartilage of the breastbone (the ancients considered the abdomen the seat of melancholy); abnormal anxiety over one's health

ALSO: hypocrisy, hypocrite, hypothetical

IN, IM, IL, IR (1)
in, into

insect [IN in + SECT to cut]—a small invertebrate with a body cut into three segments (head, thorax, and abdomen); any other small invertebrate

induce [IN into + DUC to lead]—*lit.* to lead into; to persuade, as to induce someone to do something

innate [IN in + NAT to be born]—born in one, as innate good nature

incur [IN into + CUR to run]—*lit.* to run into; to bring upon oneself, as to incur a debt

ALSO: illumine, impede, incandescent, incisive, induct, infer, irrigate, insidious, inspect, invoke

IN, IM, IL, IR (2)
not

intangible [IN not + TANG to touch]—*lit.* not capable of being touched; incapable of being perceived or identified, as intangible benefits

immobile [IM not + MOB to move]—not able to move; not able to be moved

inclement [IN not + CLEMENS mild]—not mild; stormy, as inclement weather

impunity [IM not + PUN to punish]—freedom from punishment, as to act with impunity

ALSO: illicit, impervious, inadvertent, incredible, inept, infidelity, infinite, insatiable, insuperable, irreverent

INFRA beneath

infrared—designating rays just beyond the red end of the spectrum, which have a penetrating heating effect

infrasonic—designating a frequency of sound below that audible to the human ear

infrastructure—an underlying (beneath) structure; the basic facilities necessary for the functioning of an organization, community, or state, such as roads, power plants, and transportation systems

INTER between

interstate—between states, as an interstate highway (in contrast to intrastate, which is within a state)

intermediary—one who acts as a mediator between persons

interim—a time between periods or events

interferon [INTER between + FERIR to strike]—*lit.* striking each other; a protein that is produced by cells in response to a viral infection and that interferes with (strikes) viral growth

ALSO: intercede, intercollegiate, interject, interlocutor, interloper, interlude, intermittent, internecine, interurban, intervene

INTRO, INTRA
within

introduce [INTRO within + DUC to lead]—*lit.* to lead within (society); to bring in; to present

intramural [INTRA within + MUR wall]—*lit.* within the walls; within a school or college, as intramural sports (in contrast to intercollegiate, which is between colleges)

intravenous [INTRA within + VEN vein]—within a vein, as intravenous feeding

introspective [INTRO within + SPEC to look]—looking within one's mind, as an introspective mood

ALSO: introspection, introvert

ISO equal

isometric [ISO equal + METR measure]—having equal measurements

isometrics [ISO equal + METR measure]—a method of physical exercise in which one set of muscles is tensed in opposition to another set of muscles or to an immovable object

isosceles—having two equal sides, as an isosceles triangle

isotherm [ISO equal + THERM heat]—a line on a map connecting points having equal temperatures at a given time

ALSO: isobar, isotope

-ITIS inflammation

appendicitis—inflammation of the appendix

tonsillitis—inflammation of the tonsils

arthritis [ARTHR joint + -ITIS inflammation]—inflammation of the joints

bronchitis—inflammation of the broncial tubes

ALSO: dermatitis, hepatitis

JECT, JAC
to throw

reject [RE back + JECT to throw]—*lit.* to throw back; to refuse to accept

abject [AB away + JECT to throw]—*lit.* thrown away; cast down; wretched, as abject poverty

dejected [DE down + JECT to throw]—*lit.* to be cast down; depressed

trajectory [TRA across + JECT to throw]—the curved path of something hurtling through space, as the trajectory of a comet

ALSO: dejection, eject, inject, interjection, jet, jetsam, jettison, projectile, subject

JUNCT to join

juncture—the point where two things are joined; a crisis or turning point

adjunct [AD to + JUNCT to join]—something joined to another thing in a subordinate position

conjugal [CON together + JUNCT to join]—*lit.* of the joining together of husband and wife; of marriage, as conjugal vows

junta—a group of military officers or others joined together to hold political power

ALSO: conjunction, injunction, junction

JUR to take oath

jury—a group of people who take oath to give a true verdict

jurisprudence—the science of law

abjure [AB away + JUR to take oath]—*lit.* to swear away; to renounce, under oath, rights or allegiance or opinions, as to abjure one's beliefs

conjure [CON together + JUR to take oath]—originally, to be sworn together in a conspiracy; now, to summon a demon or spirit by oath or magic spell

ALSO: adjure, jurisdiction, juror, perjury

LEG law

legitimate—conforming to the law

illegal [IL not + LEG law]—prohibited by law

legislature—a group of persons empowered to make laws for a country or state

legacy—something given to a person (by law) through a will

ALSO: illegitimate, legal

LITH stone

Paleolithic [PALE ancient + LITH stone]—relating to the second period of the Stone Age when rough or chipped stone implements were used

Neolithic [NEO new + LITH stone]—relating to the latest period of the Stone Age when polished stone implements were used

lithography [LITH stone + GRAPH to write]—the art of writing or making designs on stone

megalith [MEGA large + LITH stone]—a huge stone, especially one used in prehistoric monuments

ALSO: lithograph, monolith, monolithic

LUC light

lucid—clear, easily understood, as a lucid explanation

pellucid [PER through + LUC light]—*lit.* letting maximum light shine through; exceptionally easy to understand, as pellucid prose

translucent [TRANS through + LUC light]—allowing the light to pass through partially, as frosted glass is translucent

elucidate [E out + LUC light]—to make clear by explanation, as to elucidate a passage of prose

ALSO: lucidity, luster, lustrous

MAGN great

magnitude—greatness of size, extent, or importance

magnate—an influential (great) person, especially in business or industry

magnanimous [MAGN great + ANIM spirit]—*lit.* great in spirit; generous, as a magnanimous donor

magnum opus [MAGN great + OPUS work]—a great work; the greatest achievement of an artist or writer

ALSO: Magna Charta, magnanimity, magnificent, magnify

MAN, MANU hand

manual—done by hand, as manual labor

manacle—handcuff

maneuver—originally, to work with the hands; now, to handle skillfully

manipulate—to operate by skilled use of the hands; also, to change by unfair means to suit one's own purposes

ALSO: emancipate, manage, mandate, mandatory, manicure, manufacture, manuscript

MAR   sea

submarine [SUB under + MAR sea]—a ship designed to operate under the sea

marina—a harbor with docks for small boats

maritime—on or near the sea, as maritime provinces

ultramarine [ULTRA beyond + MAR sea]—a vivid blue pigment made from powdered lapis lazuli, which was brought "from beyond the sea"

ALSO: aquamarine, mal de mer, marinade, marine, mariner, mermaid

MATER   mother

matriarch [MATER mother + ARCH ruler]—a woman who rules a family or group

alma mater [ALMA nourishing + MATER mother]—fostering mother; the college or school that one attended

matrix—a substance within which something originates, develops, or is contained; a womb; in computer science, the network of intersections between input and output leads, functioning as an encoder or decoder

matrilineal [MATER mother + LINE line]—the line of descent traced through the mother instead of through the father

ALSO: maternal, maternity, matriculate, matrimony, matron, metropolis, metropolitan

MEDI   middle

medieval [MEDI middle + EV age]—belonging to the Middle Ages

mediocre—*lit.* in the middle between good and bad; of moderate to low quality; average

mediator—one who serves (in the middle) between conflicting parties to reconcile their differences, as the mediator in a quarrel

Mediterranean [MEDI middle + TERR earth]—a body of water in the middle of dry land

ALSO: immediate, median, mediate, mediocrity, medium

MEGA   great, large

megaton—a unit of explosive force equal to a million tons of TNT

megalomania [MEGA great + MANIA madness]—a mental disorder characterized by delusions of grandeur

megalopolis [MEGA large + POLI city]—an area of cities in such close proximity as to be considered one urban complex

megabyte [MEGA large + BYTE a group of adjacent binary digits often shorter than a word that a computer processes as a unit]—a million bytes

ALSO: megalith, megaphone

META change, beyond

metabolism [META beyond + BOL to throw]—the chemical and physical changes of a substance within the living body

metaphor [META change + PHEREIN to bear]—*lit.* transfer; a figure of speech in which a word that ordinarily means one thing is used of another thing to suggest a likeness, as the evening of life

metaphysics [META beyond + PHYSICS] (so called because Aristotle's treatise on the subject came *after* his treatise on physics in his complete works)—the branch of philosophy that seeks to explain the nature of being or reality

ALSO: metamorphosis

MICRO small

microbe [MICRO small + BIO life]—a microscopic living organism such as a bacterium

micrometer [MICRO small + METER measure]—an instrument for measuring minute distances such as the thickness of a hair

microcosm [MICRO small + COSM universe]—a representation of the world on a small scale

microfiche [MICRO small + FICHE card]—a sheet of microfilm containing a number of pages in reduced form

ALSO: Micronesia, microphone, microscope, microwave

MORT death

immortal [IN not + MORT death]—living or lasting forever

mortuary—a place where dead bodies are kept before burial

mortify [MORT death + FAC to make]—*lit.* to make or cause to die; to humiliate

mortgage [MORT death + GAGE pledge]—*lit.* a dead pledge, because the pledge becomes dead (void) to one or the other of the contracting parties according as the money is, or is not, forthcoming; a temporary pledge of property as security against a debt

ALSO: amortize, mortal, mortality, mortician, postmortem, rigor mortis

MULTI many

multiplicity [MULTI many + PLIC to fold]—*lit.* having many folds; a large number, as a multiplicity of ideas

multilateral [MULTI many + LATER side]—having many sides; involving more than two nations

multifarious [MULTI many + FAC to make]—made up of many parts or kinds; having great variety, as multifarious duties

multitudinous—existing in great numbers

ALSO: multicolored, multiflora, multiform, multilinear, multiple, multiply, multipurpose, multitude

NAV ship, to sail

naval—pertaining to a navy

navigate—to steer a ship or aircraft

navigable—wide or deep enough to be traveled on by ships

nave—the central part of a church, so called because of the medieval comparison of a church to a ship

ALSO: circumnavigate, navigation, navy

NEO new

neon—"the new gas"; a colorless, odorless gas used in electric lights

neophyte [NEO new + PHYT plant]—*lit.* something newly planted; a beginner, as a neophyte at golf

neoclassicism—*lit.* the new classicism; a revival of classical forms in art, music, and literature

ALSO: Neolithic

NOM law, order

astronomical [ASTR star + NOM law]—relating to the science of the laws of the stars; enormous, as an astronomical cost

economy [ECO home + NOM law]—*lit.* home law or household management; the careful management of income

taxonomy [TAX arrangement + NOM law]—*lit.* the law of arrangement; the classifying of organisms in established categories, as the taxonomy of herbs

ergonomics [ERG work + NOM law]—*lit.* the law or rule of work; the relationship between humans and the machines and equipment they use, as the ergonomics of office furniture

ALSO: astronomy, autonomic, autonomous, autonomy, Deuteronomy, metronome

NOV new

novice—a person new to a field or activity, as a novice at cooking

novitiate—the period of time served as a novice

innovate [IN in + NOV new]—to bring in new ideas; to introduce something new

nova—a star that suddenly increases in brightness and then decreases again

ALSO: innovation, novel, novelty, renovate

OMNI all

omnivorous [OMNI all + VOR to eat]—*lit.* eating all; eating both animal and vegetable substances; also, taking in everything available, as an omnivorous reader

omnipotent [OMNI all + POT to be able]—all-powerful

omniscient [OMNI all + SCI to know]—all-knowing

omnibus—public conveyance for all (now shortened to bus); also, a collection, as a volume made up of all kinds of literature

ALSO: omnipresent

ONYM, ONOMA
name

synonym [SYN together + ONYM name]—*lit.* a name that goes together with another name; a word similar in meaning to another word, as *large* and *big*

antonym [ANTI opposite + ONYM name]—a word that is opposite in meaning to another word, as *large* and *small*

homonym [HOMO same + ONYM name]—a word pronounced like another word but having a different spelling and meaning, as *hear* and *here*

onomatopoeia [ONOMA name + POIE to make]—the making of a word (name) by imitating the natural sound associated with it, as buzz, hiss, cuckoo, chickadee, tinkle

ALSO: acronym, anonymous, patronymic, pseudonym

ORTHO straight

orthodontist [ORTH straight + ODONT tooth]—a dentist who straightens teeth

orthopedics [ORTHO straight + PED child]—*lit.* child straightening; a branch of surgery dealing with the treatment of skeletal deformities, diseases, and injuries

orthodox [ORTHO straight + DOX opinion]—*lit.* having straight opinions; conforming to accepted opinions or beliefs, especially in religion

orthography [ORTHO straight + GRAPH to write]—*lit.* straight writing; correct spelling

PARA beside

paranoid [PARA beside + NOUS mind]—having a mental disorder characterized by delusions of persecution or of grandeur

parable [PARA beside + BOL to throw]—*lit.* a story thrown beside something; a simple story illustrating a moral lesson

paraphrase—*lit.* one phrase beside another; a restatement of a passage in different words to clarify the meaning

paraprofessional—a worker who isn't a member of a given profession but who works beside the professionals

ALSO: paradigm, paradox, paragon, parallel, parameter, parasite, parenthesis, parody

PATER father

paternal—fatherly

paternalism—the governing of people in a fatherly way, especially without giving them responsibility

patrimony—inheritance from a father or ancestor

patron—*lit.* a father; one who supports or protects, as a patron of the arts

ALSO: paternity, paternoster, patriarch, patronize, patronymic

PED child
(See p. 86 for PED
meaning *foot.*)

pediatrics—a branch of medicine dealing with the child
pedagogue [PED child + AGOG leader]—originally, a
  slave who led a Greek child to school; now, a teacher
pedagogy [PED child + AGOG leader]—the art of
  teaching (leading a child)
pedant [from pedagogue]—one who pays undue attention to book learning
ALSO: orthopedics, pediatrician

PEL, PULS
to push

repel [RE back + PEL to push]—to push back; to reject,
  as to repel an offer
dispel [DIS away + PEL to push]—*lit.* to push away; to
  get rid of, as to dispel fear
expulsion [EX out + PULS to push]—a pushing out, as
  the expulsion of a people from their homeland
compulsive [COM together + PULS to push]—being
  pushed or forced from within, as having a compulsive
  desire for neatness
ALSO: compel, compulsion, expel, impel, impulsive,
  propel, pulsate, pulse, repulsive

PEND, PENS
to hang, to weigh

pending—*lit.* hanging in the balance; undecided, as a
  decision that is pending
pensive—*lit.* weighing (ideas); quietly thoughtful, as a
  pensive mood
dispense [DIS out + PENS to weigh]—to weigh out;
  to give out, as to dispense medicines
compensate [COM with + PENS to weigh]—*lit.* to weigh
  one thing against another; to make up for, as loyalty
  may compensate for lack of ability
ALSO: appendix, compendium, expend, pendant, pendu-
  lum, pension, propensity, recompense, spend, stipend

PER through

pervade [PER through + VAD to go]—*lit.* to go through;
  to spread throughout, as an odor pervades a room
perceive [PER through + CAP to take]—to take note of
  through the senses; to grasp mentally
perspicacity [PER through + SPIC to look]—the ability
  to see through something; keen understanding
pertinacious [PER through + TEN to hold]—*lit.* holding
  through; holding firmly to some purpose; stubbornly
  persistent
ALSO: impervious, per annum, perception, peregrination,
  perennial, permit, perspective, perspicacious

PERI around, near   periphery [PERI around + PHER to carry]—the outer-most part of a region within a precise boundary; environs or outskirts

peripheral—in computer science, an auxiliary device, such as a printer or plotter, that works in conjunction with the computer but is separate from it

periscope [PERI around + SCOP to look]—an instrument enabling one to look around an angle, as a periscope in a submarine

peripatetic [PERI around + PATEIN to walk]—concerning the philosophy of Aristotle, who walked around in the Lyceum of Athens while teaching; walking around from place to place; moving from place to place, as living a peripatetic life

ALSO: pericardium, perigee, periodic, perimeter, periodontal

PHOT light   photography [PHOT light + GRAPH to write]—*lit.* light writing; the process of producing images on a film by the action of light

telephoto [TELE far + PHOTO (photograph)]—a camera lens system that gives a large image of a distant object

photosynthesis [PHOT light + SYN together + THES to put]—*lit.* to put together from light; formation of sugars in the chlorophyll-containing cells of plants exposed to light

photogenic [PHOTO (photograph) + GEN birth]—*lit.* giving birth to a good photograph; attractive as a subject for photography

ALSO: photocopy, photophobia

PHYSI nature, natural   physics—the science of natural things such as matter and energy

physiology [PHYSI nature + -LOGY study of]—the biological science dealing with life processes

physiognomy [PHYSI nature + GNOM to know]—the art of judging (knowing) human character from facial features; facial features, especially when regarded as revealing character

physique—the body considered with reference to its proportions, muscular development, and appearance

ALSO: metaphysics, physical, physician, physiotherapy

PLAC to please

complacent [COM with + PLAC to please]—pleased with oneself; self-satisfied

placate—*lit.* to please; to quiet the anger of, as to placate a person one has offended

implacable [IM not + PLAC to please]—not capable of being pleased or pacified; relentless

placebo [(Latin) PLACEBO "I shall please"]—a harmless but useless medicine given to please or humor a patient; also, an inactive substance used as a control in an experiment

ALSO: placid, pleasure

PLIC, PLEX, PLY
to fold

complex [COM together + PLEX to fold]—*lit.* folded together; involved; complicated

complicity [COM together + PLIC to fold]—*lit.* folded together (with wrongdoers); partnership in wrongdoing, as accepting stolen goods is complicity in theft

duplicity [DU two + PLIC to fold]—*lit.* folding twice; double-dealing

implicate [IM in + PLIC to fold]—to involve; to show a connection with a crime or fault, as a thief's confession may implicate others

ALSO: accomplice, complicate, deploy, display, explicit, multiply, perplex, pliant, replica, triplicate

POLI city

politics—the methods of managing a government (city)

politic—prudent or shrewd, as a politician might be

police—the official force established to maintain order in a city

metropolis [MATER mother + POLI city]—*lit.* mother city; a main city

ALSO: acropolis, cosmopolitan, megalopolis, metropolitan, necropolis, policy, politician, polity

POLY many

polygon [POLY many + GON angle]—a figure having many angles

polygamy [POLY many + GAM marriage]—the practice of having more than one mate at a time

polytheism [POLY many + THE god]—a belief in many gods

polytechnic [POLY many + TECHN skill]—providing instruction in many scientific and technical subjects

ALSO: polychromatic, polygamist, polyglot, polygraph, polymorphic, polyphonic

PON, POS
to place, to put

exponent [EX out + PON to put]—*lit.* to put forward; one who sets forth ideas, as an exponent of free trade

component [COM together + PON to put]—*lit.* something that is put together with something else; a part

depose [DE away + POS to put]—*lit.* to put away; to remove from office

interpose [INTER between + POS to put]—*lit.* to put between; to put in as an interruption, as to interpose a new idea into the discussion

ALSO: composure, compound, depository, expose, indisposed, opponent, postpone, preposition, proponent, propose

PORT to carry

portable—capable of being carried

transport [TRANS across + PORT to carry]—to carry across from one place to another

portage—the carrying of boats overland from one body of water to another

deportment [DE off + PORT to carry]—the way one carries oneself; behavior

ALSO: comport, deport, deportee, disport, export, import, porter, portfolio, report

PROB to prove, honest

probation—a trial period in which a person proves fitness for membership in a working or social group; the suspension of a sentence of one convicted of a minor offense on condition of good behavior

probate—the legal proving of a will as genuine

approbation—official approval

probity—complete honesty; integrity

ALSO: approve, probable, probe, proof, prove, reprobate, reprove

PROTO first

prototype—an original (first) model on which others are patterned

protoplasm—the essential (first) living matter of all animal and plant cells

proton—an elementary particle found in the nucleus of all atoms

protocol [PROTO first + KOLLA glue]—originally, the first sheet glued to a papyrus roll bearing a table of contents; the forms of ceremony observed by diplomats

ALSO: protozoa

PSEUD   false

pseudo—false; pretended; sham, as a pseudoathlete

pseudoscience—an unscientific method presented as scientific

pseudonym [PSEUD false + ONYM name]—*lit.* a false name; a pen name

pseudopodium [PSEUD false + POD foot]—*lit.* false foot; a temporary projection of the protoplasm in organisms such as the amoeba, serving as a means of locomotion and of taking in food

PSYCH   mind

psychic—pertaining to the mind and extrasensory mental processes such as extrasensory perception and mental telepathy

psyche—the soul; the mind

psychosomatic [PSYCH mind + SOM body]—pertaining to a disorder of the body caused or aggravated by the mind

psychogenic [PSYCH mind + GEN birth]—originating in the mind or in mental or emotional conflict, as a psychogenic illness

ALSO: psychedelic, psychiatry, psychoanalysis, psychology, psychopathic, psychosis, psychotherapy

PYR   fire

pyromaniac—one who has an uncontrollable impulse to start fires

pyrotechnics [PYRO fire + TECHN skill]—a fireworks display; a brilliant display

pyre—a pile of combustibles for burning a corpse as a funeral rite in some countries

pyracantha [PYR fire + ACANTH thorn]—the fire thorn bush (with red berries)

ALSO: Pyrex

QUADR, QUART
four

quart—a fourth part of a gallon

quarter—a fourth part of a dollar

quadruplets—four offspring born in a single birth

quadrangle—a rectangular area surrounded on all four sides by buildings, as on a college campus, and informally called the quad

ALSO: quadrant, quadrilateral, quadrille, quadriplegic, quadruped, quarto, quatrain

REG, RECT
to rule, straight,
right

regent—one acting in the place of a ruler; a member of a board governing an institution such as a university

regime—a government that is in power; a social system

rectify—to make right or correct, as to rectify an error

rectitude—moral uprightness

ALSO: correct, erect, rectangle, regal, regalia, regimen, regiment, region, regular, regulate

RETRO backward

retroactive—applying to a prior period, as a retroactive law

retrogression [RETRO backward + GRAD to step]—a return to a more primitive state

retrograde [RETRO backward + GRAD to step]—moving backward to an earlier or inferior condition, as taking a retrograde step

retrospection [RETRO backward + SPEC to look]—looking back or reviewing the past

ALSO: retrospect

RUPT to break

disrupt [DIS apart + RUPT to break]—*lit.* to break apart; to throw into confusion or disorder

erupt [E out + RUPT to break]—to break out; to burst forth, as ashes from a volcano or teeth through the gums

rupture—a breaking apart or separating, as the rupture of a blood vessel or the rupture of peaceful relations between countries

corrupt [COR together + RUPT to break]—deteriorated from the normal or standard; marked by immorality, dishonesty, or bribery, as a corrupt court

ALSO: abrupt, bankrupt, incorruptible, interrupt

SAT enough

satisfy [SAT enough + FAC to do]—to do enough; to fill a need or desire

satiate—to satisfy with more than enough, as to satiate one's appetite

insatiable [IN not + SAT enough]—not ever getting enough, as an insatiable desire to travel

saturate—to soak thoroughly or more than enough

ALSO: dissatisfaction, sate, satiety

SCOP to look

scope—the extent of one's view, thought, or actions

microscope [MICRO small + SCOP to look]—an instrument for looking at small objects

horoscope [HOR hour + SCOP to look]—looking at the position of the stars and planets at the hour of a person's birth

stereoscope [STER solid + SCOP to look]—an instrument through which two pictures of the same scene are viewed, one by each eye, to give a three-dimensional (solid) effect

ALSO: episcopal, kaleidoscope, periscope, stethoscope, tachistoscope, telescope

SEMI half

semifinal—*lit.* halfway to the final; a competition preceding the final event

semitropical—having some of the characteristics of the tropics

semiconscious—half-conscious

semidetached—attached to something on one side only, as a semidetached house

ALSO: semiannual, semicircle, semicolon, semiconductor, semiformal, semiprecious, semitrailer

SENT, SENS
to feel

sentiment—tender feeling

consent [CON together + SENT to feel]—*lit.* to feel together; to agree

sentient—having sensation or feeling

presentiment [PRE before + SENT to feel]—a feeling beforehand; a foreknowledge, as a presentiment that something is going to happen

ALSO: consensus, dissent, insensate, resent, scent, sensation, sensitive, sensitize, sensory, sensuous

SEQU to follow

sequel—a continuation; a result or a consequence

sequence—a following of one thing after another

consequence [CON (intensive) + SEQU to follow]—something that logically follows from an action or condition

obsequious [OB to +SEQU to follow]—much too willing to follow or obey; overly submissive

ALSO: ensue, inconsequential, persecute, sequential, subsequent

SOL (1) sun

solar—relating to the sun, as solar heating

solarium—a room exposed to the sun

solstice—the time when the sun is either farthest north or farthest south of the equator

SOL (2) alone

sole—being the only one

solo—a performance by one person alone

solitude—the state of being alone; a lonely or secluded place

desolate [DE completely + SOL alone]—*lit.* completely alone; lonely

ALSO: soliloquy, solitaire, solitary

SOLV to free,
to loosen

solve—*lit.* to loosen; to clear up; to explain

solvent—*lit.* free (of debt); able to pay one's debts; a liquid capable of dissolving another substance

absolve [AB from + SOLV to free]—to pronounce free from guilt or blame

dissolution [DIS apart + SOLV to loosen]—a breaking up, as the dissolution of a business association

ALSO: dissolve, insoluble, insolvent, resolute, resolve, solution

SOPH   wise

sophisticated—having worldly wisdom
sophomore [SOPH wise + MOR foolish]—*lit.* a wise fool;
  a second-year high school or college student
sophomoric—immature and overconfident
sophistry—clever but misleading reasoning
ALSO: philosopher, philosophy, sophist

SPIR   to breathe

inspire [IN in + SPIR to breathe]—*lit.* to breathe into;
  to stimulate to some creative effort
conspire [CON with + SPIR to breathe]—*lit.* to breathe
  with; to plan together secretly
aspire [AD to + SPIR to breathe]—*lit.* to breathe toward
  an end; to have a great ambition
expire [EX out + SPIR to breathe]—*lit.* to breathe one's
  last breath; to die
ALSO: aspiration, inspiration, perspiration, perspire,
  respiration, respiratory, spirit, transpire

TANG, TACT,
TIG, TAG
to touch

tangible—capable of being touched, as tangible assets
tact—*lit.* having the right touch in handling difficult
  situations
tangent—a line touching but not intersecting another
  line; a sudden change of course, as going off on a
  tangent
contiguous [CON with + TIG to touch]—touching on
  one side, as contiguous states
ALSO: contact, contagious, contingent, contingency, in-
  tact, intangible, tactful, tactile, tax

TECHN   art, skill

technology [TECHN skill + -LOGY study of]—the science or study of the practical or industrial arts; a
  scientific method of achieving a practical purpose
technician—an expert in a technical process
technocracy [TECHN skill + CRAC to rule]—a government controlled by technicians
technicality—a minute detail of some art or skill that only
  an expert would be aware of
ALSO: architect, polytechnic, pyrotechnics, technical,
  technique, technophobia

TEMPOR   time

tempo—the time or rate of speed of a musical passage;
  rate of motion; pace, as the hectic tempo of modern life
extemporaneous [EX out + TEMPOR time]—*lit.* without time; performed with no preparation, as an extemporaneous speech
temporal—limited by time; concerned with wordly affairs
  in contrast to spiritual ones
temporize—to act evasively in order to gain time or postpone a decision
ALSO: contemporary, pro tem, temporary

TEN, TIN, TAIN
to hold

tenor—in music, originally, the voice that held the melody; now, the highest male voice; the meaning held in something written or spoken, as the tenor of his argument

tenure—a permanent hold on a position, as faculty tenure

tenacious—holding firmly, as a tenacious grip

tenet—a belief that one holds

ALSO: detain, lieutenant, pertinacious, sustain, tenable, tenacity, tenant, tenement, tentative, untenable

TEND, TENS,
TENT   to stretch

tension—mental or emotional strain; a strained (stretched) relation between persons or groups

tent—a portable shelter of canvas stretched over poles and ropes

ostensible [OB before + TENS to stretch]—*lit.* stretched out before one; apparent; professed, as an ostensible purpose

pretentious [PRE before + TENT to stretch]—claiming (stretching for) distinction; making an extravagant outward show, as a pretentious way of speaking

ALSO: attention, contend, détente, distend, extend, extensive, hypotenuse, pretend, tendency, tetanus

TERR   earth

territory—an area of the earth

terrier—a small dog, so named because it digs in the earth after animals in burrows

terrestrial—pertaining to the earth; living or growing on the earth

terrain—the physical features of a tract of land

ALSO: disinter, extraterrestrial, inter, Mediterranean, subterranean, terrace, terra cotta, terra firma, terra incognita

THE, THEO   god

theology [THEO god + -LOGY study of]—the study of religion

theocentric—having God as the central interest and ultimate concern, as a theocentric universe

enthusiasm [EN in + THE god]—*lit.* having a god within one; inspired feeling for a subject or cause

apotheosis [APO from + THEO god]—making a god from a person or thing; deification, as the apotheosis of an emperor

ALSO: atheist, Dorothea, monotheism, pantheism, pantheon, polytheism, theism, theocracy, Theodore

THERM   heat

thermometer [THERM heat + METER measure]—an instrument for measuring heat

thermal—using, producing, or caused by heat

thermos—a bottle or jug for keeping liquids at their original temperature for several hours

thermodynamics [THERM heat + DYN power]—the branch of physics that deals with transforming heat into other kinds of energy

ALSO: diathermy, isotherm, thermonuclear, thermostat

TOM to cut

appendectomy—cutting out the appendix

anatomy [ANA up + TOM to cut]—originally, a cutting up or dissecting of a body; now, a study of the structure of the body

atom—[A not + TOM to cut]—once considered the smallest particle of matter that could not be cut or split

dichotomy [DICH two + TOM to cut]—division into two sharply opposed groups, as the dichotomy between theory and practice

ALSO: entomology, epitome, tome, tonsillectomy

TRACT to drag, to draw

tractor—a powerful vehicle used for pulling machinery

tractable—able to be drawn; therefore easily managed or controlled, as a tractable child

intractable [IN not + TRACT to draw]—*lit.* not able to be drawn; difficult to manage, as an intractable child; difficult to relieve or cure, as intractable pain

protracted [PRO forward + TRACT to draw]—drawn out; prolonged, as a protracted meeting

ALSO: abstract, attract, contract, detract, distract, extract, protractor, retract, subtract, traction

TRANS across

transfusion [TRANS across + FUS to pour]—*lit.* the pouring of blood across from one person to another; the injection of whole blood into the bloodstream

transitory—passing quickly across; fleeting, as a transitory hope

transcend [TRANS across + SCEND to climb]—to rise above, as hope transcends experience

intransigent [IN not + TRANS across + AGERE to act] refusing to compromise or come to an agreement

ALSO: transcribe, transgress, transient, transit, translate, translucent, transmute, transparent, transpire, transverse

ULTRA beyond

ultraviolet—beyond the visible spectrum at its violet end

ultrasonic [ULTRA beyond + SON sound]—pertaining to acoustic frequencies above the range audible to the human ear

ultrasound—a technology using ultrasonic sound, as for medical therapy

ultramodern—*lit.* beyond modern; extremely modern

ALSO: ultramarine

UMBR   shade

umbrella—a circular canopy carried to give shade or protection from rain

umbrage—*lit.* a shadow of suspicion or distrust; offense; resentment, as to take umbrage at a remark

penumbra [PEN almost + UMBR shade]—a partial shadow, as in an eclipse, between regions of complete shadow and full light

adumbrate [AD to + UMBR shade]—to give a sketchy outline of; to foreshadow in a vague way, as to adumbrate the plans for reorganizing the department

UNI   one

unison [UNI one + SON sound]—*lit.* having one sound; a speaking or singing together

unanimous [UNI one + ANIM mind]—of one mind; having the same opinions

unilateral [UNI one + LATER side]—affecting only one side; obligating only one of two or more parties or nations

unicorn—a mythical horse with one horn projecting from the forehead

ALSO: unanimity, unicellular, unification, uniform, unify, union, unique, unity, universe, university

URB   city

urban—relating to a city, as urban renewal

interurban [INTER between + URB city]—between cities

suburb [SUB under, near + URB city]—an outlying (near) part of the city

urbane—having the refined manners of city society

ALSO: exurbanite, exurbia, suburbanite, urbanity

VAC   empty

evacuate [E out + VAC empty]—to empty out; to make empty, as to evacuate a building

vacation—*lit.* empty of work; freedom from work; a holiday

vacuous—empty; devoid of meaning; stupid; dull, as a vacuous expression

vacuity—total lack of ideas; emptiness of mind

ALSO: vacancy, vacant, vacate, vacuum

VEN   to come

advent [AD to + VEN to come]—the coming or arrival, especially of something awaited; (cap.) the birth of Christ

invent [IN on + VEN to come]—*lit.* to come upon; to think up or imagine; to create for the first time

intervene [INTER between + VEN to come]—to come between as an influencing force, as to intervene in a quarrel

eventuate [E out + VEN to come]—to come out finally; to result, as the talks between labor and management may eventuate in a compromise

ALSO: adventitious, adventure, circumvent, convene, event, invention, inventory, revenue, souvenir, venture

VERB word

verbal—concerned with words
verbose—wordy, as verbose writing
verbiage—an excess of words; wordiness
verbatim—in exactly the same words, as to print a speech verbatim
ALSO: adverb, proverb, verbalize

VIC, VICE
  substitute

vice president—one who substitutes for the president
viceroy [VIC substitute + ROI king]—a governor of a country ruling as representative of the king
vicar—one serving as a substitute for another
vicarious—performed or endured by one person substituting for another; experienced through imagined participation in another's experience, as a vicarious thrill
ALSO: vice admiral, vice-regent

VID, VIS to see

video—the visual portion of television as distinguished from the audio
visa—an endorsement on a passport showing that it has been seen by the proper officials
improvise [IM not + PRO before + VIS to see]—*lit.* not to see beforehand; to produce without preparation
envision [EN in + VIS to see]—to see in the mind; to imagine, as to envision a coming event
ALSO: invisible, evident, provident, provision, revise, supervise, television, visionary, visor, vista

VIV to live

vivid—colorful; lifelike, as a vivid description
vivacious—full of life; lively
vivify—to give life to; to make more lively or striking
vivisection [VIV to live + SECT to cut]—the cutting into a living animal for scientific research
ALSO: convivial, revive, survive, survivor, viands

VOL to wish,
    to will

volunteer—one who serves of one's own free will
voluntary—done of one's own free will
volition—an act of willing, choosing, or deciding, as doing something of one's own volition
involuntary [IN not + VOL to will]—not performed willingly; not subject to control; automatic
ALSO: benevolence, benevolent, malevolent

VOLV   to roll

revolve [RE back + VOLV to roll]—to spin or turn around a center

devolve [DE down + VOLV to roll]—*lit.* to roll down; to pass on to a substitute or successor, as it now devolves upon the new employee to finish the job

volume—a book, called a volume because the first books were rolls of parchment

voluble—characterized by a great flow (rolling out) of words; fluent

ALSO: convoluted, evolution, evolve, involve, revolution, voluminous

ZO   animal

zoology [ZO animal + -LOGY study of]—the science that deals with animals

zodiac—that part of the sky through which the sun seems to move; so called because its 12 constellations resemble animals

protozoa [PROTO first + ZO animal]—the first forms of life; single-celled microscopic organisms

zooplankton—floating, often microscopic, aquatic animals

ALSO: spermatozoon, zoo

REVIEW TEST Here's a test on a few of the 164 roots in the last part of the text. Put a C in front of each sentence in which all words are used correctly. Look up any word you miss in the Word Index (p. 193) to find the page where it is defined.

_____ 1. They were lucky to have inclement weather on their entire trip.

_____ 2. We lived a peripatetic life in those years, moving from one state to another.

_____ 3. Climbing that mountain was so energizing that I had to go to bed afterward.

_____ 4. His ostensible reason was that he was busy, but of course we knew that wasn't his real reason.

_____ 5. He was appointed corpulent manager of a large corporation.

_____ 6. We wanted to plant a couple of deciduous trees that wouldn't shed their leaves in the winter.

_____ 7. Her omnivorous taste in literature led her to read widely.

_____ 8. Waves of nostalgia swept over me as I walked past the old house.

_____ 9. The students in the math class were having trouble with infractions.

_____ 10. It takes more than urbane manners to make up for a vacuous mind.

_____ 11. She's pertinacious in lobbying for returnable bottles.

_____ 12. His bellicose disposition made him unpleasant to work with.

_____ 13. Her effusive praise was more than we cared for.

_____ 14. At the beginning of my talk I recapitulated my main points.

_____ 15. The professor's incisive remarks always went straight to the point.

_____ 16. The cult leader was tenacious in sticking to his beliefs.

_____ 17. It was only an egregious error and hardly worth mentioning.

_____ 18. Our new neighbors are affluent; they even drive three cars.

_____ 19. My friend was always ready to take umbrage at any criticism.

_____ 20. The new employee was obdurate and eager to cooperate.

_____ 21. My dad is the epitome of unselfishness.

_____ 22. The lecturer elucidated the subject until it was clear to all of us.

_____ 23. The boss has an insatiable desire for praise.

_____ 24. I could listen calmly to his long diatribe against me because I knew none of it was true.

Answers

p. 9 PRELIMINARY TEST

1.B	6.B	11.D	16.C	21.B	26.A
2.D	7.C	12.A	17.D	22.C	27.D
3.A	8.A	13.A	18.B	23.D	
4.A	9.B	14.B	19.A	24.B	
5.D	10.C	15.D	20.C	25.C	

p. 13 EXERCISE 1

1.amoral	4.atheist	7.atypical
2.anomaly	5.asymmetrical	8.anemia
3.agnostic	6.anecdotes	9.anarchy

p. 15 EXERCISE 1

1.ambiguous	4.ambience	7.ambidextrous
2.ambivalent	5.ambiguity	8.amphitheater
3.ambivalence	6.amphibians	9.amphibious

p. 17 EXERCISE 1

1.centennial	4.annuity	7.biennial
2.millennium	5.anniversary	8.perennial
3.annals	6.semiannual or biannual	9.superannuated

EXERCISE 2 REVIEW

1.ambience	3.atypical	5.ambivalent
2.ambiguity	4.superannuated	

p. 19 EXERCISE 1

1.antequated	4.antebellum	7.antedate
2.antediluvian	5.antiquarian	8.antecedent
3.anterior	6.antiquity	9.ante

p. 21 EXERCISE 1

1.anthropomorphic	3.misanthrope	5.anthropoid
2.anthropologist	4.anthropocentric	6.philanthropist

p. 23 EXERCISE 1

1.anticlimax	4.antibiotics	7.antidote
2.antagonist	5.antiphonal	
3.antithesis	6.Antarctica	

p. 25 EXERCISE 1

1.autocratic	3.autocrat	5.autonomic
2.automaton	4.autocracy	

EXERCISE 2 REVIEW
All sentences are correct except 2, 6, 8, 9, 11, 15, 19.

p. 27 EXERCISE 1

1.benediction
2.benefactor
3.beneficence or benevolence

4.benign
5.benevolent
6.beneficiary

7. benevolence or beneficence

EXERCISE 2 REVIEW
All sentences are correct except 1, 5.

p. 29 EXERCISE 1

1.bilateral
2.bipartisan
3.bicameral
4.bivalve
5.bisect

6.biceps
7.binoculars
8.bicentennial
9.bilingual
10.bigamy

11.bicuspid
12.biped
13.binary

p. 31 EXERCISE 1

1.biosphere
2.symbiotic

3.symbiosis
4.biopsy

5.biofeedback
6.biodegradable

EXERCISE 2 REVIEW
All sentences are correct except 3, 6, 7, 8.

p. 33 EXERCISE 1

1.chronological
2.anachronism

3.synchronize
4.chronometer

5.chronic

EXERCISE 2 REVIEW

1.chronicle
2.anarchy
3.bicameral
4.beneficiary
5.antebellum

6.anachronism
7.misanthropic
8.anthropocentric
9.autonomous
10.biopsy

11.biofeedback
12.antique
13.ambience

p. 35 EXERCISE 1

1.circumlocution
2.circumvent

3.circumspect
4.circumscribe

5.circuitous
6.circumnavigated

EXERCISE 2
We'll be glad to repair your TV set free of charge.

EXERCISE 3 REVIEW
All sentences are correct except 6, 7, 8.

p. 38 EXERCISE 1

1.commensurate
2.condone
3.correlate
4.consummate
5.compunction

6.commodious
7.commiserate
8.collusion
9.compendium
10.collaborate or cooperate

11.congenital
12.condominium
13.coherent
14.convene
15.convivial

EXERCISE 2 REVIEW
All sentences are correct except 2, 4, 5.

p. 38 EXERCISE 3 REVIEW

1.biology	BIO	life	study of plant and animal life
2.bivalves	BI	two	mollusk having two shells
3.amphibians	AMPHI	both	
	BIO	life	animals living both in water and on land
4.circuitous	CIRCUM	around	roundabout
5.biodegradable	BIO	life	capable of decaying
6.ambivalent	AMBI	both	having conflicting feelings
7.condone	CON	(intensive)	forgive
8.compunction	COM	(intensive)	prick of conscience
9.perennial	ENN	year	lasting many years

p. 41 EXERCISE 1

1.credible	4.miscreant	7.credulous
2.incredulity	5.incredulous	8.incredible
3.credence	6.credulity	9.credibility

p. 43 EXERCISE 1

1.cursory	5.discursive	9.discourses
2.concurrent	6.recourse	10.recur
3.recurrent	7.precursor	
4.concur	8.concourse	

p. 45 EXERCISE 1

1.endemic	3.epidemic	5.Demographic
2.demagogue	4.pandemic	6.demagoguery

p. 47 EXERCISE 1

1.jurisdiction	4.abdicated	7.valedictorian
2.diction	5.edict	8.addicted
3.dictatorial	6.dictum	

p. 49 EXERCISE 1

1.dissuade	5.discomfited or	8.disparate
2.disarray	disconcerted	9.dissonant
3.disburse	6.dismantled	
4.disseminate	7.disparity	

p. 51 EXERCISE 1

1.equate	5.equilibrium	9.equivocal
2.equivocated	6.equable	10.equitable
3.equity	7.equinox	
4.equinimity	8.equilateral	

EXERCISE 2 REVIEW

All answers are correct except 2, 5, 6, 7, 9, 11, 17, 19, 22, 26, 30, 32, 33.

p. 53 EXERCISE 4 REVIEW

1.incredulous	CRED	to believe	disbelieving
2.equanimity	EQU	equal	composure
3.circumvent	CIRCUM	around	get around
4.atypical	A	not	not typical
5.consensus	CON	together	general agreement
6.benefactor	BENE	good	one who gives help
7.ambivalent	AMBI	both	having conflicting feelings
8.antithesis	ANTI	opposite	the exact opposite
9.concur	CON	together	
	CUR	to run	agree
10.incredible	CRED	to believe	unbelievable

p. 55 EXERCISE 2

1. eulogized
2. euphonious
3. eulogy
4. euphemism
5. euphoria
6. euphony
7. euthanasia

EXERCISE 3 REVIEW

All sentences are correct except 2, 3, 7, 11.

p. 57 EXERCISE 1

1. enervating
2. efface
3. exonerate
4. expurgated
5. ebullient
6. emolument
7. expatiated
8. excoriated

p. 59 EXERCISE 1

1. bona fide
2. diffident
3. perfidious
4. infidel
5. fidelity
6. confidant
7. perfidy

EXERCISE 2 REVIEW

All sentences are correct except 2, 3, 6, 10.

p. 61 EXERCISE 1

1. genesis
2. genealogy
3. engender
4. progenitor
5. genre
6. progeny
7. ingenuous
8. genocide

p. 63 EXERCISE 1

1. graphic
2. monogram
3. choreography
4. topography
5. cardiogram
6. graffiti
7. monograph
8. epigram
9. calligraphy
10. graphite
11. seismograph

p. 65 EXERCISE 1

1. epilogue
2. monologue
3. prologue
4. analogy
5. dialogue
6. analogous

EXERCISE 3 REVIEW

All sentences are correct except 2, 5.

p. 67 EXERCISE 1

1. psychology
2. meteorology
3. etymology
4. geology
5. archeology
6. entomology
7. ornithology
8. embryology
9. ecology

p. 69 EXERCISE 1

1. loquacious
2. colloquial
3. grandiloquent
4. soliloquy
5. ventriloquist
6. colloquium

EXERCISE 3 REVIEW

All sentences are correct except 3, 8, 12.

p. 71 EXERCISE 1

1. malinger
2. malady
3. malcontent
4. malicious
5. malignant
6. malign
7. malice
8. malediction
9. malfeasance
10. malevolent
11. malaise
12. maladroit
13. malapropisms
14. malefactor

p. 72 EXERCISE 3 REVIEW
All sentences are correct except 1, 6.

EXERCISE 4 REVIEW

1.conventions	CON	together	the coming together of a group
2.graphic	GRAPH	to write	full of vivid details
3.democracy	DEM	people	government by the people
4.committee	COM	together	a group of people
5.consensus	CON	together	general agreement
6.ambiguous	AMBI	around	uncertain
7.engender	GEN	birth	bring forth
8.grandiloquent	LOQU	to speak	marked by a lofty style
9.eulogize	EU	good	
	LOG	speech	praise
10. malign	MAL	bad	slander
11.anticlimax	ANTI	opposite	a drop from the important to the commonplace
12.perennial	ENN	year	lasting many years

p. 75 EXERCISE 1

1.perimeter	4.kilometer	7.symmetrical
2.barometer	5.metronome	8.parameter
3.odometer	6.pedometer	9.tachometer

EXERCISE 2 REVIEW

1.disproportionate	3.cursory
2.expatiated	4.progenitor

p. 77 EXERCISE 1 REVIEW
All sentences are correct except 2, 6, 12, 14, 16, 18, 22, 23, 25, 30.

p. 79 EXERCISE 1

1.monosyllable	3.monotone	5.monolithic
2.Monotheism	4.monogamy	6.monoliths

EXERCISE 2 REVIEW
All sentences are correct except 7, 10, 12.

p. 81 EXERCISE 1

1.mesomorphic	4.endomorphic	7.metamorphosis
2.morphology	5.amorphous	
3.Morphine	6.ectomorphic	

EXERCISE 2 REVIEW
All sentences are correct except 2, 4, 6, 9.

EXERCISE 3 REVIEW

1.antequarian	3.atheist	5.dissident
2.anthropologist	4.philanthropist	

p. 83 EXERCISE 1

1.pandemonium	4.panorama	7.panegyric
2.panacea	5.Pantomime	8.pantheon
3.pantheism	6.panoply	9.panchromatic

EXERCISE 2 REVIEW
All sentences are correct except 2, 4, 6.

p. 85 EXERCISE 1

1.apathy
2.empathy
3.psychopathic

4.antipathy
5.pathological
6.pathos

7.pathogenic
8.pathology
9.apathetic

p. 87 EXERCISE 1

1.expedite
2.expedient

3.impede
4.pedigree

5.impediment

EXERCISE 2 REVIEW

1.equable
2.ingenious

3.ebullient
4.disparity

5.around
6.euphonious

p. 89 EXERCISE 1 REVIEW

1.morphology
2.etymology
3.monolithic
4.calligraphy
5.malfeasance

6.antipathy
7.pantomime
8.expedite
9.perfidious
10.ectomorphic

11.pantheon
12.demographic
13.equitable
14.panchromatic
15.philatelist

p. 90 EXERCISE 1

1.photophobia
2.phobic
3.xenophobia

4.claustrophobia
5.hydrophobia
6.acrophobia

7.technophobia

p. 93 EXERCISE 1

1.cacophony
2.polyphonic

3.saxophone
4.megaphone

5.phonetics
6.phonics

EXERCISE 2 REVIEW

All sentences are correct except 4, 8.

p. 95 EXERCISE 1

1.posthumously
2.posterity
3.preposterous

4.posterior
5.postlude
6.Postimpressionists

7.postmortem

EXERCISE 2 REVIEW

1.emolument
2.excoriate
3.disparate

4.equivocate
5.disconcerted
6.xenophobia

7.dissidents

p. 97 EXERCISE 1

1.precipitated
2.precocious
3.precedent
4.predilection

5.unprecedented
6.preeminent
7.preponderant
8.presage

9.precludes
10.prerequisite
11.prelude

p. 99 EXERCISE 1

1.prospectus
2.proclivity or propensity
3.proponent

4.protuberant
5.procrastinate
6.profusion

7.promontory
8.provident
9.profuse

p. 101 EXERCISE 1

1.recondite
2.recalcitrant
3.revert

4.resilience
5.remission
6.recluse

7.remiss
8.recant
9.redoubtable

p. 102   EXERCISE 2
All sentences are correct except 4, 8, 15, 16, 18.

p. 105   EXERCISE 1

1.ascribe	3.transcribe	5.subscribe
2.nondescript	4.conscription	6.proscribed

EXERCISE 2   REVIEW
All sentences are correct except 5, 6, 8, 10.

p. 107   EXERCISE 1

1.sedentary	5.subside	9.subsidiary
2.assiduous	6.supersede	10.obsessed
3.subsidy	7.obsession	11.assess
4.insidious	8.sedate	12.assessor

p. 109   EXERCISE 1

1.auspicious	4.introspection	7.specious
2.perspective	5.despicable	8.spectrum
3.retrospect	6.perspicacious	9.specter

p. 111   EXERCISE 1

1.subsistence	5.subjugate	9.subterranean
2.subversive	6.subliminal	10.sub rosa
3.subterfuge	7.subsumed	
4.subservient	8.subpoena	

p. 113   EXERCISE 1   REVIEW

1.proponents	PRO	before	advocates
2.unprecedented	PRE	before	never having happened before
3.chronic	CHRON	time	continuing for a long time
4.circumvent	CIRCUM	around	to get around
5.demise	MIS	to send	death
6.ecology	-LOGY	study of	study of environment
7.endemic	DEM	people	native to a certain place
8.equate	EQU	equal	to represent as equal
9.insuperable	SUPER	over	not capable of being overcome
10.consensus	CON	together	general agreement

p. 115   EXERCISE 1

1.synthesis	4.syndrome	7.syllogism
2.symposium	5.synod	8.synergistic
3.Synthetic	6.syntax	9.symbol

p. 117   EXERCISE 1   REVIEW
All sentences are correct except 3, 4, 5, 7, 14, 15, 17, 20, 24.

p. 119   EXERCISE 1

1.extort	4.distort	7.tort
2.retort	5.tortuous	
3.contortionist	6.torturous	

EXERCISE 2   REVIEW
All sentences are correct except 5, 7, 8.

p. 121   EXERCISE 1

1.Trinity	4.trilogy	7.tripartite or trilateral
2.tripod or trivet	5.trilingual	
3.trident	6.triennial	

EXERCISE 2 REVIEW
All sentences are correct except 2, 5, 7, 8.

p. 123 EXERCISE 1

1.veritable	4.verification	7.verifiable
2.veracity	5.veracious	8.verities
3.verify	6.averred	

EXERCISE 2 REVIEW

1.insidious	7.presage	13.monotheism
2.phobic	8.obsessed	14.graphite
3.subversive	9.verifiable	15.tripartite
4.cacophony	10.trivet	16.trilogy
5.ascribed	11.telepathy	17.triennial
6.veracity	12.promontory	

p. 125 EXERCISE 1

1.adversary	5.averse	9.averted
2.Obverse	6.perverse	10.versatile
3.inadvertent	7.adversity	11.aversion
4.introvert	8.adverse	12.vertigo

p. 127 EXERCISE 3 REVIEW

1.prospect	PRO	forward	
	SPECT	to look	a looking forward
2.chronic	CHRON	time	continuing for a long time
3.concur	CON	together	
	CUR	to run	to agree
4.edicts	E	out	
	DICT	to speak	official decrees
5.propensity	PRO	forward	a natural inclination
6.aversion	VERS	to turn	extreme dislike
7.spectrum	SPEC	to look	a broad range of ideas
8.panacea	PAN	all	a remedy for all ills
9.prologue	PRO	before	
	LOG	speech	an introductory event
10.posterity	POST	after	future generations

p. 129 EXERCISE 1 REVIEW
All sentences are correct except 2, 5, 6, 8, 10, 15, 24, 25.

p. 131 EXERCISE 1

1.irrevocable	5.vociferous	9.revoked
2.evoke	6.evocative	10.vocation
3.invoked	7.invocation	
4.avocation	8.convocation	

EXERCISE 2 REVIEW
All answers are correct except 3, 7.

p. 132 COMPREHENSIVE TEST A

1.B	6.C	11.C	16.D	21.C	26.C
2.C	7.A	12.A	17.D	22.D	27.C
3.D	8.D	13.C	18.B	23.C	
4.C	9.A	14.D	19.A	24.B	
5.B	10.D	15.C	20.D	25.A	

p. 134 COMPREHENSIVE TEST B
1. AMPHI both, BIO life.   an animal that lives both in water and on land; a plane that can land on water or on land
2. ANTE before.   to occur before something else
3. ANTHROP human, MORPH form.   thought of as having human form or characteristics
4. ANTI against, BIO life.   a substance used against living microorganisms
5. A not, SYM together, METER to measure.   not having both sides equal
6. AUTO self, GRAPH to write.   one's signature
7. BENE good, DICT to speak.   a blessing
8. BI two, ENN year.   occurring every two years
9. CHRON time, METER measure.   an instrument for measuring time, especially in navigation
10. CIRCUM around, SCRIB to write.   to confine
11. COL together, LOQU to speak.   informal
12. CON together, VERT to turn.   to cause to turn from one belief to another
13. CRED to believe.   believable
14. DIS apart, CUR to run.   rambling
15. E out, MISS to send.   a person sent out on a specific mission
16. EQU equal.   to represent as equal
17. EU good, PHON sound.   pleasing sounds
18. E out, VOC to call.   to call forth, as memories or feelings
19. EX out, PED foot.   *lit.* foot out of an entanglement; useful in getting a desired result
20. FID faith.   faithfulness
21. GEN race, -LOGY study of.   the study of family descent
22. MAL bad.   a disease
23. MONO one, GRAM to write.   letters entwined into one design
24. PAN all, DEM people.   widespread
25. PHIL love, ANTHROP human.   helping humanity with charitable donations
26. PHOBIA fear.   an excessive or illogical fear
27. PRE before, POST after.   absurd
28. PRO before, LOG speech.   a speech before a play; an introductory event
29. PRO forward, SPECT to look.   a summary of a proposed venture
30. RE back, TORT to twist.   to twist a remark back on the giver
31. SUB under, SID to sit.   to settle down
32. SUPER above, ANN year.   retired because of age
33. TELE far, PATH feeling.   the supposed communication of two people far apart
34. TRI three, VIA way.   unimportant matters
35. VER true.   to prove something is true

p. 137 COMPREHENSIVE TEST C
All sentences are correct except 2, 6, 16, 17, 18, 21, 23, 27, 31, 32, 33, 36, 37, 38, 50, 52.

p. 139 CHALLENGE TEST

1.C	6.A	11.C	16.C	21.C
2.B	7.A	12.A	17.A	22.B
3.B	8.B	13.A	18.C	23.C
4.B	9.C	14.C	19.A	24.B
5.A	10.C	15.B	20.C	

p. 179 REVIEW TEST
All sentences are correct except 1, 3, 5, 6, 9, 14, 17, 20.

ROOT INDEX

WORD INDEX